How To Raise An

MVP

MOST VALUABLE PERSON

How To Raise An
MVP
Most Valuable Person

Ambrose & FredaRobinson
with Steve Hubbard

ZondervanPublishingHouse
Grand Rapids, Michigan

A Division of HarperCollinsPublishers

How to Raise an MVP

Copyright © 1996 by Ambrose and Freda Robinson

Requests for information should be addressed to:

ZondervanPublishingHouse
Grand Rapids, Michigan 49530

Library of Congress Cataloging-in-Publication Data

Robinson, Ambrose, 1942–
    How to raise an MVP / Ambrose Robinson and Freda Robinson with Steve Hubbard.
      p. cm.
    ISBN: 0-310-20829-7
    1. Child rearing—United States—Case studies.   2. Parenting—United States— Case
studies.   3. Family—United States—Case studies.   4. Family—Religious life—United
States—Case studies.   5. Basketball players—United States—Family relationships—Case
studies.   6. Robinson, David, 1965–   . I. Robinson, Freda, 1939–   . II. Hubbard, Steve
(Steve A.)   III. Title.
HQ770.R63 1996
649'.1—dc 20
            96-10274
            CIP

This edition printed on acid-free paper and meets the American National Standards Institute
Z39.48 standard.

All Scripture quotations, unless otherwise indicated, are taken from the *Holy Bible: New
International Version*®. NIV®. Copyright © 1973, 1978, 1984 by International Bible Society.
Used by permission of Zondervan Publishing House. All rights reserved.

Edited by John Sloan, Lori Walburg, and Gloria Kempton
Interior design by Sue Vandenberg Koppenol

Printed in the United States of America

---

96 97 98 99 00 01 02 03 /❖ DH/ 10 9 8 7 6 5 4 3 2 1

*To all parents, who have had or will have
to go through similar experiences.—AR and FR*

*To my parents, who gave me love, discipline
and work ethic—and to my wife and two children,
who give me love, nourishment and happiness.—SH*

Contents

Acknowledgments

It would have been very difficult to write this book without the help of numerous people, family, and friends who have so generously shared their memories, words, and wisdom to help us. Writing this book was much like raising our children. It has been an educational journey. Our heartfelt thanks especially go to Kimberly, David, and Chuck. In sharing their memories of growing up, our children jogged our memories about our experiences. Our children are three of the greatest blessings we ever had, and without them, there would be no book, because we wouldn't have the experiences to share with you. We learned from them just as we learned from our parents, who gave us the foundation for our lives.

Scott Waxman, our literary agent, saw a book amid our experiences and turned that seed of an idea into a reality by connecting us with our writer and publisher.

Steve Hubbard, our writer, listened to us over the months and helped translate words for the ear into writing for the eyes.

Numerous other writers have written about David and our family over the years and their stories helped refresh our memories. The San Antonio Spurs and NBA Photos provided reference material and photos.

First-time authors could not have asked for better support than we received from John Sloan and Lori Walburg, our editors at Zondervan, who offered faith, encouragement, support, and feedback to turn our memories into what we hope will be an entertaining and educational book.

Foreword

Most people know me as the 1995 NBA MVP. They seem impressed by the way I handle myself on and off the court. But everything I've learned can be traced back to my parents. They created an environment conducive to my development as an individual and my growth as a professional athlete. They could have chosen any of their three children to write this, and so I feel privileged they allowed me to provide this foreword.

As I reflect on my childhood, many things both good and bad come to memory. Our family faced many of the same difficulties every family faces. We didn't have life on easy street. That is why I think so many people will identify with our experiences.

I remember I stole a candy bar when I was about ten. I didn't think it was any big deal. It was a big store, and they had plenty more on the shelves. My parents *did* think it was a big deal. When my father found out, he marched me down to the 7-Eleven and made me apologize in front of everyone in the place. I'll never forget the feeling I had standing behind the desk after being exposed as a thief. It left a lasting impression on me. That was my father's way of showing me what kind of person I didn't want to become. After that, stealing was no longer an option for me.

I remember another time when I was in first grade, I cut up my dad's chair. I didn't do it intentionally. I was sitting in his leather recliner, watching TV and eating something, and I was poking a kitchen knife into the arms of the chair. When I looked down, I had cut holes all over both arms of the recliner. It was one of the more expensive items in the house, and we didn't have a lot of excess money. I still remember the spanking; I learned a lesson about being careless and defacing other people's property.

That kind of strict, disciplined parenting is even more important now. Families in our society today are faced with a growing number of challenges. Children are pressured daily to try or sell drugs. There is more pressure than ever before to enter into sexual relationships at an earlier age, and they confront crime and violence that are growing at alarming rates. Many parents are too busy living their own lives to make sure their children are living the right lives. Some are more preoccupied with work, hobbies, and self-improvement than with giving their children the quality time they need and deserve.

The family unit is being attacked at its very foundation. But without the family, our country has no strength. As the strength of the family grows, so grows the strength of our communities and the strength of our nation. Everything starts in the home. We need to be more concerned parents. Our children need to be more attentive, caring, and disciplined.

Just as my parents provided me with a positive environment, I want to provide the best environment possible for my family. I have been blessed with a loving wife, Valerie, and two wonderful sons, David Jr. and Corey. The Lord has entrusted me with their lives, and I don't plan on letting him down. The examples I learned from my parents and the lessons God is teaching me through the Bible and daily prayer guide me and set the stage for what I hope will be a strong family.

My parents laid the foundation. If we ever went astray, they got us back on course. But they were pro-active, as well. Instead of waiting for something to happen, they were active in preventing, directing, and guiding. My dad always had a vision for who he wanted me to be. Parents have to know where they want their kids to go. That doesn't mean making them into something they're not, but it does mean giving the kids a direction, a purpose. The parents need a focus in raising their kids.

My parents gave us vision, motivation, discipline, and loving kindness. They have, I believe, many wonderful things to give you. Some of it might be funny, some of it might be sad, some of it might be advice, but hopefully, all of it will be helpful and encouraging. They wrote this book out of care and concern.

12

Those who know anything about my life and the effect my mother and father had on my life, know my parents care. Their advice in the following pages is motivated by a genuine care to see all parents do better.

I hope you will enjoy the ideas put forth in this book, because they have indeed proven to work for us. It is my sincere desire that those of you who read this book will not just walk away with some amusing stories and anecdotes about the lives of the Robinson family, but will sense the genuine loving care and passion that exists in our relationships.

My parents remain a big part of every big decision I make. Even at thirty, I seek their counsel. I value their counsel. I could never repay them for how much they have invested in my life.

David Robinson
San Antonio, Texas

Introduction: The Swift Family Robinson

David Robinson watched, spellbound, as his father fixed the family car. Dad amazed David. Many children found their heroes in sports or music or movies; David found his in the driveway, the living room, the back yard.

Dad played Beethoven's "Moonlight Sonata" on the piano. He put together radios and TVs out of tiny electronics kits. He taught David how to hit a baseball from both sides of the plate, how to dribble a basketball, how to hit a bull's-eye with his bow and arrow, how to roll strikes at the bowling alley, how to choose the right kind of bait depending on the fish. And now here he was, sliding under the car, solving yet another problem.

David was ten or twelve, and he'd gone to gifted-student classes since third grade, but he couldn't understand all this.

How could one man know so much about *everything*?

"Did you go to Dad School or something?" he asked his father.

Ambrose Robinson could be the father of "Dad Schools" all around the country. He and his wife Freda could teach us all about how to raise an MVP. Not just a Most Valuable Player, but a Most Valuable Person, too.

Because if you're a parent, you want your child to grow up to be David Robinson—or to marry him. He is a role model not just because "The Admiral" is basketball's quickest, most versatile center, but because he neither smokes nor drinks, because he preaches the virtues of church and school and the vice of sex and drugs, because he's smart and multitalented and the ultimate success story, whether you're talking backboards, keyboards or college boards.

The San Antonio Spurs center is the National Basketball Association's reigning Most Valuable Player and perhaps its Most Valuable Person. He is an officer and a gentleman, a real Renaissance man: classical pianist, jazz saxophonist, brilliant student, calculus whiz, computer genius, Naval officer, Olympics Dream Team hero, born-again Christian. And, oh yes: A philanthropist who tithes ten percent of his salary and makes countless motivational speeches to organizations focusing on family, faith, and children.

David is no family fluke. His two siblings are success stories in their own right. Older sister Kimberly already holds a bachelor's degree in marketing and a master's in business administration. She juggles two jobs while working on her doctorate so she can go from part-time to full-time college professor. Younger brother Chuck graduated from the Naval Academy and started for the Midshipmen basketball team, just like David. A first lieutenant in charge of supplies and logistics at Kessler Air Force Base in Biloxi, Mississippi, Chuck is on schedule to become a licensed minister in June 1996 and an Air Force captain in 1997. All three children, just like their mother, have given their lives to the Lord and practice the values they preach.

David Robinson spurred the Spurs to the NBA's best record in 1994–95, just as he spurred short and slow Navy underdogs to their greatest heights when he was an All-American and college basketball's consensus Player of the Year. An All-Star each of his six seasons, he's also been honored as the NBA's Rookie of the Year, Defensive Player of the Year, scoring champion, rebounding champion, and shot-blocking champion. He was voted one of the NBA's top three centers and one of its top two defensive centers every season, and he's won the award for best overall statistical season four of those six years. David will become the first male basketball player to appear in three Olympics Games as the Dream Team goes for another gold this summer in Atlanta.

But beyond the basketball court, David also represents everything we want from our children, from our heroes. In an era when so many of us turn to our sports stars only to find them sadly lacking, David Robinson is a true hero, a true role model.

"Whatever success I've achieved, I owe to my parents," David says. "Not just some of it, but all of it. Obviously, the Lord gave me my abilities, but my ability to not only handle but excel at so many things comes from the way I was raised. There were times when I might not have made the right decisions or I might not have had enough personal drive to be the best player I could be, but my parents were always there for me. I've gone from not even being a player in high school to being the Most Valuable Player of the National Basketball Association. At so many points along the way, I could have stopped. They gave me the drive to continue to improve. It's a testimony to their character and what they instilled in me. In a day when good parents are scarce, they stand out."

For all his fame and fortune, David values faith and family ahead of all else. He credits his father for just about everything that has made him successful: his intelligence, competitiveness, curiosity, worry-free attitude, and varied interests in learning, reading, math, music, sports, and computers. He still reminds his father of the day he asked about Dad School, and he turns to Ambrose even more often now that he has two boys of his own.

"I patterned myself after my dad. I never had sports role models. The only person I ever saw anything in was my dad. I've often wondered how he came up with all the right answers," he says, and shakes his head.

"You just think, 'Man, how could he have a general knowledge of *everything*?' People ask me now, 'How are you good at everything? You go bowling, you golf, you play music, you do this, you do that. How in the world can you do everything?' I got that from my dad. He was into everything. You don't want to just have a working knowledge. You want to be good at what you do. Everything we put our hands in, we want to excel at. Everything we touch, we compete at. Not just sports. Anything you can think of, anything we do. We have fun with it, but it's competition."

Freda swells with pride as she recounts how often her children tell her she is "the best mom in the world." Then as now, they weren't just trying to butter her up. They meant it.

"We have the best mother, without a doubt," Chuck says. "I always wanted to go everywhere with my mom. Not necessarily because she bought me stuff, but because she helped me do everything. She did it because she loved me, and she didn't expect anything in return. I enjoy her more now than ever. We have a great time.

"She is great; my dad is great. He taught us how to be men, how to take care of business, how to be true to our word, how to be places on time. The Bible says, 'In business, be as men.' It means just do everything the way it's supposed to be done. That's what he taught us. My mom taught me how to be a person. Just love people and be nice and say please. That combination molded us. My father taught us how to be men and my mother taught us how to be people. They did a great job of balancing discipline and instilling the right values in our lives. I pray I can raise my kids like my parents did. They did a phenomenal job."

When he has children, Chuck says he will raise them exactly the same way, and Kimberly says she'll heap on the same strong doses of discipline, education, and responsibility.

"They did what every parent should do: They raised us, nurtured us, guided us, gave us hope, gave us a vision," she says. "They encouraged us. They pushed education. They instilled responsibility. I used to think people had children just to make them work. My father would say, 'I'm giving you these chores so you can learn to be responsible.' I used to think, 'No way. You just want someone to bus dishes. You have a live-in dishwasher.'

"By the time I got in high school, I could have raised five kids by myself. But Dad was right; it did teach me responsibility. When I went away to college, I was more than prepared."

What can you learn from this Swift Family Robinson?

They offer parenting insights and success solutions that obviously worked while entertaining you with stories about David Robinson, a true superstar on and off the court.

No jargon, no philosophical preaching, no chapters titled "Why Punishment Doesn't Work." Just a no-nonsense, common-sense approach that gets results.

All three children have grown up to be smart, successful, well-rounded adults. That David Robinson became the NBA's MVP is merely a bonus. "Most of all," his mom says, "I like the person he is." Ambrose and Freda Robinson raised three Most Valuable Persons—and so can you.

Part One
Birth Through Preschool

Chapter One

The Miracle and the Blessing

<hr>

*Freda and Ambrose Robinson believe
God saved David Robinson's life and gave
him great basketball talent so that he might
share his money and his message of faith.*

Long before he could run and dunk and block shots like no
other player in basketball—why, before he could even walk—
David Robinson nearly died.

Let's let his parents tell the story:

FREDA It was February of 1966, and we were living in Newport,
Rhode Island, when the Navy sent Ambrose to South
America on the *U.S.S. Van Voorhis*. I decided to take the kids
and go visit my sister, Jessie, in Rye Beach, New Hampshire,
only 128 miles away. The weather forecast had predicted an ice
storm, and Ambrose told me not to go. But it didn't look that
bad, so I took Ambrose to the ship and left for New Hampshire.

We had been there a couple of days when we woke up to an
ice storm. There was no school, and if they cancel school in
New Hampshire, you know it's bad weather. Kim was nearly
three years old and David was six months old, and my sister had
six children, so you can imagine the noise level.

I got David out of his portable crib and left him on the bed
while I went to the kitchen to heat his bottle. I started talking

to Jessie and forgot I had left the baby on the bed. He stopped crying, and I thought he had fallen asleep. So I talked with her for a few more minutes, then went in the bedroom, but I didn't see him on the bed, and I didn't see him on the floor. I thought my brother-in-law had taken him to his room to play.

I knocked on his door and said, "Mitch, do you have David?"

He said, "No."

I said, "Don't kid me. He needs his bottle and I can't find him."

He came out in his housecoat and said, "Freda, I don't have him."

I said, "You're serious? Well, where is he?" I went into the living room and asked all the kids, "Is David here?"

They said, "No, ma'am."

I said, "Well, where *is* he?"

I went back to the bedroom and looked all over and finally saw the tip of his head. He had scooted toward the wall and had gotten hung up in the space between the mattress and the wall, and it had cut off his circulation. His nose was mashed up against the mattress and he couldn't breathe.

I ran and picked him up, and he had turned blue. I grabbed him and started screaming, "He's dead! My baby is dead!" I just knew he was dead.

My sister came into the room and said, "Stop it! Look, he *will* be dead if you don't give him CPR."

I was a nurse, and I knew CPR, but I told her, "I've never done it on a human. I've only done it on a mannequin. I can't do it."

She said, "If you don't want him to die, you better try."

So I laid him down on the bed and opened up his airway. I swept his mouth with my fingers to see if he had anything in his mouth, and he didn't. I listened and couldn't hear him breathing. I gave him four quick breaths, and I thought I saw his chest expand.

Jessie said, "It looks like he's breathing."

I picked him up and his little eyes rolled back in his head as if he had no control, and I was afraid he was going into convulsions. I knew the cold would shock him, so I ran through the kitchen and out into the garage. His eyes stopped rolling then, but his little body was cold and he started to cry.

Meanwhile, my brother-in-law had called for an ambulance. They had a warning out: No vehicles on the highway unless it's an emergency. By the time the emergency crew got there, I had wrapped David in blankets and was trying to establish body temperature again.

When they came in the house, they said, "Is this the house that called about the baby? Where is the baby?"

I said, "This is the baby."

They couldn't believe this was the same baby who had been blue and not breathing, and they said, "Whatever you did must have worked. He's just cold now."

They put him in the ambulance, took him to the hospital, and put him in an isolette, trying to get his body temperature back up.

I was worried about brain damage. It's supposed to occur four to six minutes after a person stops breathing. They wanted to know how long he had gone without oxygen, and I told them I didn't know. When you're afraid, the minutes seem a lot longer than they really are. I must have been out of the room at least five minutes, but I didn't know how long he had been in distress.

It was just a miracle I went in the room when I did.

The technology wasn't as advanced then as it is now. The doctor told us there was nothing they could do to tell if he was brain damaged because they didn't know how long he had gone without oxygen.

I said, "You mean I'll have to wait until he starts learning or talking?"

He said, "That's about the size of it."

And so we lived with that fear. It was stressful living with the unknown and feeling guilty about it. I knew I was at fault. I had no business leaving him alone on the bed. It was double jeopardy. I was told not to go in the first place, and then this happened.

AMBROSE I found out about David's scare in letters while I was away at sea. That was frightening enough, but I was also upset because I had told her not to go to New Hampshire with the ice storm coming. That same week, she wrecked my car.

FREDA The accident happened two days after I gave David CPR. I was taking my sister to the shopping center, and a lady ran into me on the ice. The weather was still bad, and I had no business going to the shopping center, but my sister wanted to go. A lady slid into our car and tore up one whole side—David's side. He was just lying on the front seat by me. We didn't have car seats then, and he didn't have a seat belt on. But he was fine.

I was a nervous wreck. I knew I had to tell Ambrose, but I did not want to hear "I told you so." When he got the letter and was able to call, he said, "Are you hurt? Is David hurt? Did Jessie get hurt?"

I said, "Nobody got hurt. The car is just destroyed."

He said, "I'm so glad none of you got hurt," and that really made me feel better, because the last thing I needed was to be reminded of where I should have been.

I lived with that worry about brain damage until David was three and I found out he could read. He wasn't just reading pictures, he was reading words. He was normal. We just counted our blessings.

AMBROSE We don't know how long David stopped breathing. We don't know how close he came to dying, but we do know the Lord works in strange and mysterious ways.

David has some special talents, and we believe the Lord left him on this earth for a special reason. He does a lot of ministering now. He signs autographs with a scripture verse. He speaks to people about faith. He's an ambassador of sorts.

He reaches people because of basketball, but his purpose goes beyond basketball. What he can accomplish with his ministry is more important than anything he can accomplish in basketball. He could be the next Billy Graham. I could foresee in five or ten years he could have numerous followers as does Billy Graham and the 700 Club.

FREDA I don't know if he'll become the next Billy Graham, but I do know he will help a lot of people through his ministry. Now, that doesn't mean he'll have a big, plush church somewhere. But he is so effective in his ministry now, and he's the type of vessel that produces and gets results.

I think—I *know*—the Lord allowed David to live for a reason. When David speaks to youth and different audiences, he captivates them. He's so soft-spoken, so genuine, so unselfish. He's been a blessing to so many people, not only financially, but spiritually. I could probably use ten words to describe him, but the word blessing describes him better than anything.

When I look at David's children, I think what a blessing they are to him, but he and his wife are a blessing to them, too. He has a nice family and they're happy and they love each other. God has blessed him in his career, but the thing I feel good about is that he can still do something when basketball is over. He won't be finished.

He's chosen. Sometimes the Lord gives you insights. I knew when David started breathing that day, it had to be the Lord. I knew there was a mission. The whole time I was doing CPR, I was screaming and praying, "Lord, don't let my child die." The Lord magnified his life for me. He gave me the blessing I asked for.

Chapter Two
The Greatest Gift of All

*Children are precious. They deserve
your best effort.*

Every parent should view every child as a blessing, a gift from God. Because children are the legacy you leave, the greatest accomplishment you can ever achieve. They are, actor Peter Ustinov said, "the only form of immortality we can be sure of." Or, as a poet once wrote:

Fifty years from now
  It will not matter
What kind of car you drove
  How much you had in your bank account
Nor what your clothes looked like
  But the world will be a little better
Because you were important
  In the life of a child

Any male can father a child, but it takes a real man to become a dad. When you give birth to a child, you take on a lifelong responsibility. This is a commitment not to be taken lightly, though far too often in today's society, it is. Parents abandoning their children, be it literally or figuratively, is not a new thing. Nearly seventy years ago, Judge Leon Yankwich wrote, "There are no illegitimate children—only illegitimate parents." But today we face a sad epidemic, a plague of children having children, of parents spurning their obligation to their offspring.

FREDA We wrote this book because we looked around and saw a lack of real love and discipline, caring and consistency. If any of our advice can work for you, we'll feel we have succeeded. It's our sincere hope that you can raise an MVP, too.

AMBROSE These deadbeat dads, I just can't see it. We need to take care of our responsibilities. When we bring children into the world, we're responsible for them at least until they're eighteen.

I can't knock single parents because some are alone through no fault of their own, some because of the nature of their jobs. For instance, when our children were younger, I was gone a lot because of my Naval duties. I'd be gone as far as South America and the Mediterranean. Out of 365 days a year, Freda was around 250 more than I was. So when I was home, I made sure I spent most of my free time with my family. We'd fish, bowl, go crabbing, go on vacation, play all kinds of sports.

It's important for both parents to be there whenever they can. Certainly, it's more difficult being a single parent. Still, children can survive if they get good parenting, regardless of the number of parents or the kind of neighborhood. You can read success stories every day of children who escaped the ghetto. What's scary are the gangs. If a child doesn't get attention from a parent, he'll find it somewhere else. If he finds it in a gang, it could lead him down the wrong path. In the ghetto, more kids succumb to gang pressure, but you *can* make it out. It's more about parenting than neighborhood. The only weapon you have is to be a good parent, a loving parent.

FREDA When you choose whether to stay at home with your children or put them into day care, you have to think about what's quality time and what's quantity. Even one hour of quality time a day with your child makes a difference.

I've done it all ways: I've stayed home full time, I've worked full time, I've worked part time. I don't regret working. If I had small children and could afford to stay home, I would do it. But how many households today don't need two salaries?

All you can do is your best. But are you doing that? Here are a few questions to ask yourself to see how you measure up as a parent:

Am I teaching my children real values?

Am I parenting in a way that pleases God?

What do I do when my children need me? Do I always make myself available to them?

How do I communicate with them?

What can I do to listen to them more thoroughly and evaluate a situation before I act?

Am I involved in their education, or am I leaving it all up to the school?

How much time do I spend with my children?

How many times have I put my children to bed recently?

How many times have I read any bedtime stories to them recently?

How many times have I prayed with them recently?

When was the last time I dressed my children?

When was the last time we had dinner together as a family?

How many times have I hugged my children and said "I love you" lately?

Am I being an example of what I am teaching my children?

Chapter Three

Parenting Basics: It All Starts with Love

Love is what you do *for your children.*

You can be smart and successful in your career and your marriage and still feel overwhelmed when you bring a newborn into the home. Figuring out how to raise children, especially the first one, can make you feel like a bumbling idiot. What do you know? What do you do? Where do you start?

First, calm down. You know more than you think, and when you don't know something, don't be afraid to pick up the phone or the baby book. Your friends and family want to help. Let them. The baby books and doctors and nurses can answer questions and ease doubts. Let them.

You begin with love, unconditional love. Love isn't just a feeling, isn't just mouthing some words. Love is what you *do* for your children. It doesn't mean you do everything, doesn't mean you buy everything, doesn't mean you say it all the time. You show your love by doing things for your children, but also by saying no. You show your love by establishing discipline, setting goals and limits, guiding, molding, caring, securing, nurturing, instilling values, setting an example, and instilling confidence.

As the child grows old enough to understand, you sprinkle in discipline. In the first couple of years, this might just mean

31

helping the child sleep through the night by not running to him every time he wakes up. As the years go by, discipline takes on greater importance. Discipline is training that molds, guides, corrects, and perfects your children's mental faculties and moral character.

Ambrose and Freda Robinson believe if you love your children, you must give them discipline.

FREDA The basics of raising children are love, prayer, discipline, security, and education. Love is the main thing. Love and prayer. Some people don't rank prayer as highly as I do. I've been called a lunatic before, so if people disagree, that's fine. I'm talking about what worked for me.

Love can be defined in many ways, but I find this to be true: Love is giving of yourself. That's all love is. Most parents would say they love their children, but what you *do* for your children shows how much you love them. That doesn't mean to spoil them. You have to draw the line. You shouldn't give all yeses and no nos.

Hungry children are looking everywhere for love. If they're not loved, they're vulnerable. They fall prey to those who would abuse them. We can say they're looking for attention or looking for trouble, but they're really looking for love. Not necessarily for people to say, "I love you," but to show they care.

Children want adults to care enough about them to discipline them. Sometimes if they don't get that discipline in their own home, they'll look for it elsewhere. When we lived in Virginia Beach, this child would come into our home, jump on our bed, stand up in our chairs, and just generally misbehave. His mother gave him everything. His home was beautiful. His parents had adopted him because they couldn't have children. They were so happy to have him, anything this child wanted, they bought him. Ambrose would discipline him along with our children, and he didn't even get mad. It was like he was glad we told him no.

Children are looking for love *and* discipline. A lot of times, a child may be thinking, "I want somebody to talk with me. I want some attention." He's so starved for attention, he'll do something bad, just to get it. That means that child needs more love.

Without love, discipline is void. If you punish a child and you're doing it for any other reason than that you love that child, then there's something wrong with you, and *you* need to be punished.

Children need to be taught values, real values.

AMBROSE You can't assume children will pick up the correct values when they grow up. A sense of values comes via responsibility. We have to practice what we preach.

FREDA That's probably near the top of the list of basics: Setting an example. You have to guide the child and not let the child guide you. You should make the decisions. You won't always make the right decision; we all make mistakes. But if you love your children, they will forgive you for your mistakes.

AMBROSE Yes! You have to be the example. Don't go around complaining and gossiping and blowing your top about every little thing, because your children will follow your example.

Along those lines, I've always used positive language. There were no such words as "I can't" in my household. I told our children that numerous times: "There is absolutely nothing you can't do. If you don't *want* to do it or you don't have the time, that's a different story."

I also didn't say, "I *have* to do something." That implies somebody else is making you do it, and you're doing it for reasons other than your own. You've heard the saying; the only thing you *have* to do is die and pay taxes.

FREDA You should have love and a vision for each child. That vision will help shape and mold a child into becoming successful, which is every parent's dream. Without a vision, you can lose your sense of direction sometimes.

33

You also have to teach your children to be honest, even when they think honesty isn't the best policy. This is true of us as adults, too. I remember when I was a nurse and sick of working the swing shift, and always changing hours, and I asked if I could take a day job.

The interviewer asked me, "What's your priority? Your family or your job?"

I said, "My family first, my job second."

She looked at me and sighed.

I thought, "Oh, I won't get the job now. Why did I tell the truth?"

She said, "I've got a lot of applicants for the job who are just as qualified as you. I'll call you in two days."

After I thought about it, I decided, "I don't care if I get the job; at least I didn't lie."

She called the next day and said, "We chose you. I liked you. I liked your honesty."

Chapter Four

Teach Your Children Well

─────────

Make education your children's highest priority.

The Robinsons were leaving Key West, tooling up U.S. Highway 1, when a revelation struck.

David stood up in the back seat, peered over his father's shoulder and proclaimed, "Daddy, you're speeding."

"No, I'm not," Ambrose fibbed.

Whereupon David pointed out that the speed-limit sign read fifty-five mph and the odometer read sixty.

Ambrose and Freda gave each other "Can you believe this?" looks and were filled with equal parts relief and wonderment. Why, they didn't have to worry about brain damage anymore. Their little boy was three years old—and he could read!

FREDA I knew then there was nothing wrong with this child. We couldn't believe he could read that young.

We read to him a lot, but that wasn't the only way he learned. An educational TV show in Key West promoted Dr. Seuss books, and we probably bought every one of them. David and Kim would get out their little chairs and books and sit in front of the TV and follow along with the TV host. Kim was in first grade and David wasn't even in school. They'd listen and read along, and that reinforced what they were reading.

AMBROSE We made a game of reading and learning. We traveled a lot, and we'd have the kids reading road signs and license plates and telling me the types of cars and that type of thing.

Education was the thing we stressed the most. If you can make it in sports, great, but not many people do, and most likely, you'll need to fall back on your education. Without an education, you can't do anything. With a *proper* education, you can do anything you want to do.

In their first few years, a lot of it was learning by doing. Show and tell. Show and demonstrate. David would watch me, and he was inquisitive. That's why he became so good with his hands, with tools and electronics. Even today, he'll take things apart just to see how they work.

You can't just tell a child to do something and expect him to do it without knowing how. Explaining why helps kids understand the rationale. Chuck always asked why. The other two didn't; it was blind following. I got away with "Because I said so" for a long time. I wouldn't with today's kids. I'd explain more of the reasons why.

FREDA We stressed education from Day One. You can't start too soon. All the research says much of what children become is based on what is learned those first two years. Talking with them, communicating with them is probably Step One. That includes reading, telling night-time stories, saying prayers at bedtime. As they learn to talk and understand, you start defining words for them. You move on to simple sentences. You read to them. We ordered all these educational books early on. A two-year-old will say, "Read it to me," and it's important to do it, because they listen and learn. They look at pictures and associate them with words. They learn at an earlier age than we have any idea.

I don't really believe in teaching A-B-C-D-E-F-G in order, just singing the letters. I believe in teaching kids to know the letters when they see them. They need to know the different

36

letters, the different numbers. We used flash cards to teach the alphabet, addition, subtraction, and multiplication.

As soon as they begin to read, you want to teach them to comprehend, not just to call words. That was a big thing for us: Anybody can call out words, but real reading is knowing what you've read. Put the book down and tell me what it means.

I tried to buy a lot of guidance toys. We'd buy toys they had to figure out. We bought bright colored toys because primary colors catch their attention. You want an area in the house for learning time. You want a chalkboard to write on, a bulletin board so you can put up little notes, and a yardstick to point to things and show the kids how to measure. They like charts with bright colors on them. You can teach a lot with foods. Let them count the fruit. Or count the crackers. Learning to count is more attractive if they can eat the food afterwards.

Chapter Five
Almost Divorced

Nourish not only your baby but your spouse, too, if you want your marriage to thrive.

Key West was sunny and pretty and quaint, but Freda was fed up. She was working long hours at the hospital, sometimes double shifts, and coming home dead tired only to raise two toddlers by herself more often that not. She resented her husband going off to sea—it seemed his ship left every time the wind blew—and then coming home and changing the rules she'd established. Kimberly was four and David was two, and Freda felt that Ambrose's intervention totally confused the children.

Freda would try to talk to Ambrose and he wouldn't answer, and she'd get furious and stop talking, and then tempers would flare some more. His Navy buddies would come over for weekend picnics and try to see who could drink the most beer, and Freda decided she wasn't going to take it any longer. Frazzled, she turned to a nurse's aide for advice. She knew Liz had gone through a divorce, and she said she thought that was what she wanted.

"Things can't be that bad," Liz said.

"I'm just tired of this," Freda said.

"Did he hit you?" Liz asked.

"Oh, no, he's not crazy. I'm just tired," Freda said.

"Divorce is no picnic," Liz replied. She knew Ambrose. She liked Ambrose. "Your husband has a nice place for you," she told Freda. "He's a good provider. He loves you and your kids. Why do you want to get rid of him?"

"It's not that I want to get rid of him," Freda answered, "but I'm just tired. I can't handle this."

Liz said, "You know, they don't just give you divorces for no reason."

"They don't?" Freda said, surprised. She thought she could get a divorce automatically, as long as she had the money to pay for it.

Liz tried to talk her out of it, but a couple of small disagreements had turned Freda's temper raw, and she insisted. Finally, Liz said, "Since you insist on this, I'll recommend one of the best lawyers in town. If anybody will be fair, he will be. He makes sure you warrant a divorce. I don't think he'll recommend one, though."

Freda called her mother and told her she was leaving Ambrose.

"You can't do that," her mother scolded. "It's not right."

Freda knew her mother and father liked Ambrose even more than Liz did, but she still asked if they'd help pay for the divorce.

"I'm not sending you money to leave him unless Ambrose tells me it's okay," her mom replied. "I'm not taking your side because I know you have a bad temper. If he did anything, you incited him."

"I thought you cared about me," Freda pouted. "You won't even take my word."

Her mom said, "You tell him to call me. If I hear both sides, if he's in agreement, then I'll help. But I'm not sending any money to separate you. I'm not doing it."

Still, Freda called the lawyer's office, and when the secretary told her it would be two weeks before she could get an appointment, Freda replied, "Oh, no, no, no, no. I have to see him very soon."

"Is it that urgent? Is it a matter of life and death?"

"Yes," Freda said.

The secretary said, "In that case, can you be down here in two hours? I'll squeeze you in just before lunch."

"I'll be there," Freda said.

And so, she was waiting when the lawyer returned from court. The secretary told him Freda had an urgent problem. Freda told him she wanted a divorce, and the lawyer got out his tape recorder.

"This is routine," he said. "I always tape the conversation when a spouse comes in without the partner. I don't want you to be embarrassed, but I'm going to have your husband come, and I'll play this for him. So tell me the truth, because you'll have to listen to it again—in front of him."

"Okay, I don't have anything to hide," Freda said, and she explained all her problems.

He looked at her as if she were wacky.

"I've heard everything you've just told me, and you don't have a problem," he said.

"*What*?" Freda shouted.

He said, "You have a miscommunication problem, and I believe this is one of the few cases where I can help."

Now it was Freda's turn to look at him as if he were crazy.

He said, "I'll tell you what I'm going to do. You go home, and I'll send your husband a letter."

"He's not going to listen to you," Freda butted in.

He said, "*You* listen to me. Sometimes we can talk too much. I want you to go home and go on as normal, but when he gets this letter, I want both of you to come in on Saturday. Don't argue a lot. If he asks you if you saw me, tell the truth."

Ambrose got the letter the next day, read it and announced, "I'm not going anywhere."

"Okay," Freda said and nothing more. She knew she was going, and she knew the attorney would start divorce proceedings if Ambrose didn't show up. She woke up Saturday morning, got herself and the children ready, and told Ambrose she was going.

He said, "Just hold up. I'm going, too. We'll ride down together."

She wanted to drop the children at the baby-sitter's. He wanted to take them to the attorney's office so they could "see where their mother has us going."

The attorney saw the children in the outer office and said, "Oooh, these are the two children? They're precious." He told his secretary to give them some cookies and take care of them while he spoke with their parents inside his office. He asked Ambrose to listen to Freda's tape and tell him if she had told the truth.

After listening, Ambrose said, "It's a little exaggerated, but she told the truth."

The attorney said, "Do you want to save this marriage?" and Ambrose said, "By all means."

He asked Freda, "Do you want to save it?" and she hedged, "Yes, I guess so."

The lawyer lectured them for forty-five minutes, then told them, "I have two sons who were pilots in the Navy, and it's hard on a service family because you're separated so much. Then just the turmoil of two people blending their ideas together. That's hard, too."

He turned to Ambrose. "I have a lot of respect for Freda because she's a nurse, and she gets out and works and helps you. I have a lot of respect for a woman who helps her husband. So she's got some things going for her. You have two young children. They need both parents. If she comes back down here, I'll give her her wish. But right now, you two don't need a divorce. You have a communication problem. You have to find a way to talk to each other. You need to talk more."

As they were ushered out, Ambrose asked, "How much do we owe you?"

The lawyer said, "Nothing. It's a pleasure to help two people stay together. But if you come back, it'll cost you big time."

They left—and they never went back.

The moral of the story: Even the most ideal marriages face bumps in the road, and as wonderful as babies and toddlers can be, they place vast and seemingly never-ending demands upon their parents' time, energy, and finances. Once they are born, the couple's lives change forever. Children add a new layer of stress and responsibility, and the parents must learn to cope with the changes. They cannot neglect their children, but they also cannot neglect their relationship if they are to keep the marriage strong.

FREDA Children make a big difference in your life. When they come into a marriage, your time is stretched a little more, it's elasticized, and it can lead to stress. Your husband—the child you can't control—sometimes feels the kids are getting more attention than he is. If that's not carefully dealt with, it can lead to problems.

You can be overworked, overloaded, and tempers get short. If you have two temperatures flare up, it causes combustion. I have a lot of patience, but I'll be the first to admit, when rubbed and rubbed and rubbed, I can explode. You can get to the point where you feel, "Would I be better off married or unmarried? Could I do better by myself?" It happens to the best of us. People should know this is normal.

AMBROSE After David was born, we probably came closest to divorce as we ever have. We had some real ups and downs. But we were able to work it out, and as we found out later, that helped us communicate much more effectively. You really need to talk about it. It's not "Whose way is right?" so much as "Which way is effective for this situation now?" Both ways could be right, but what works now?

FREDA It was hard to go public with our personal problems, but we both learned from the experience. We started talking. We didn't argue. We just talked. We started listening to each other and to our children.

If couples are having problems, they should talk—and listen—to friends or family or counselors. If they go to a divorce lawyer, I hope they get one like I found. It could have been one just looking to make money who would have given me a divorce. Seeing that lawyer probably helped us more than anything in this world.

Time together as a family is important. But you've got to do some things to make you and your spouse happy, too. You've got to do some things without the kids. We'd get a sitter and go to a hotel across town for a little vacation. We did a lot of things to try to brighten our marriage. I look back and it doesn't seem like thirty-some years. It seems like ten.

Chapter Six

Don't Just Dictate, Communicate!

Communication is two-way. You need
to talk and listen.

How many times have you found yourself barking orders at your children, only to see them resist and defy your drill-sergeant routine and get everyone even more frustrated?

Think about it: Do you respond better when someone bosses you around, or when someone explains what needs to be done, describes how it can be done, and gives you some choices so you feel you have input?

Whether with adults or children, the trick is in learning how to communicate with one another; better to persuade people to cooperate than to risk temper tantrums and raised blood pressure.

FREDA We don't listen to our children. We want to exhibit we're adults and we're the authority. But that's not what it's really about. I don't need to say, "I'm the boss, I work, I call the shots." I need to sit down and listen to my children. They're small adults, and sometimes we don't let them have a voice. You'll hear children say, "Won't you listen to me? You're not listening."

If we want good communication with our kids, we need to listen to them. We have to be friends as well as parents.

We should praise our children frequently for kind deeds, the way they look, the accomplishments they achieve. That plays a big part in self-esteem. We should praise and compliment for the least little positive thing. Our children need to hear us say, "I love you." Every day we need to hug our children and kiss our children and show them in no uncertain terms, "I care." We need to show them as well as tell them.

If we have to criticize, we should make it constructive criticism. It's not always easy, but we have to remember they have feelings just like we do. It's how we phrase our criticism, what tone of voice we use.

AMBROSE I was strict, more of a disciplinarian, whereas Freda would talk and try to reason with the children. They knew they could talk their mom into things, but they knew when I said something, they were to do it. I'd give in occasionally, but not very often.

If I could do it over, I'd listen a little more. I'd recommend that to any parent. Listen to your children. They might wear on you, but listen and find out what they're saying. You have to establish that line of communication, so they know they can talk to you.

Chapter Seven

Temper Tantrums

---

*Teach your children how to manage
their anger.*

Children are bound to get feisty and frustrated when they
don't get their way, and their parents are usually the ones to
incur their wrath. Different solutions work for different children at different times at different ages.

You can start by building a warm, trusting relationship
with your children. You can ask about their day and accentu-
ate the positive by asking about the favorite thing they did that
day. You can spend quiet time with them, reading a favorite
book or sharing stories. You can let them know that no one's
perfect, that anger is natural for everyone.

Show them how you cope with your own stresses, and suggest outlets. Maybe an aggressive boy who's slapping his siblings
or friends needs to pound out his frustration by hammering
wooden pegs on a pounding board, or pummeling a drum set or
a miniature punching bag, or simply punching a pillow or a
mattress. Maybe, instead of taking out her frustrations on her
little brother, a big sister can knead some clay or Play-Doh,
make a "mad" picture with crayons or paint, make up a puppet
snow, or blow off steam by going for a walk or a swim or a run
around the block. Maybe the child can join in a parent's activ-

ity, whether it's as fun as playing a sport or a game or as mundane as washing the car or going to the store.

You should praise a child who is about to hit a sibling or friend but finds the self-control to stop. You can help him learn self-control by giving him activities requiring concentration, such as putting a puzzle together, stringing beads, or building blocks.

Of course, if a child is harming himself or others, you don't have time to reason. You must stop the action first. For toddlers and preschoolers, that might mean firmly but lovingly holding them and/or removing them from the problem. For older children, that might mean taking (or sending) them to a "timeout chair" or their room.

FREDA Sometimes children misbehave just to get attention, and once you correct them, they're okay. It's almost like, "I got their attention and I'm fine now." They know how to manipulate.

It's awful to say to a kid, "What is wrong with you?" or "What a stupid thing to do." But I think it's okay to say, "If you do this one more time," and then let him know what the consequences are. You need to draw a line so that he understands you're tired of his foolishness. You can try to reason with him, but if he's doing something dangerous, you need to act immediately. Say, he's throwing lye in another child's eyes. Are you going to stand there and reason—or snatch the lye out of his hands?

When children are having temper tantrums, it's because they're tired and frustrated; they're not going to listen. I've seen this happen in the grocery store. The boy is kicking up a storm. The mother says, "You've done this in the car. You've done it here. This is enough. This is the limit." The boy pops his mama in the face, and she says, "How dare you?" and he pops her again. He's out of control. She's supposed to reason with the child while she gets popped in the face six times? No way!

If David were having a temper tantrum, I would look at him and say, "Get up now. Stop this. It's not acceptable." I could talk to him, and most likely, it wouldn't happen again. Now Chuck, I would have to show him. Chuck is from Missouri. He wouldn't believe me, wouldn't take me seriously. I would have to help him up. Both would go to their rooms, but I had to manually get Chuck up and let him know what was next. Chuck had a little temper that was more outward than David's. He would pout until I had to give him a light spanking, and only then would he believe he'd get a spanking if he pulled that stunt again.

I can remember Kim throwing only one tantrum on me. I didn't agree with her about some problem she had with the boys, and she got mad and fell down on the kitchen floor. I couldn't believe it; that wasn't Kim. I said, "Look, get up and get up now. This very instant. We're not having this. You're not having your way."

She got up and her little eyes got big. She couldn't believe I was talking bad to her. She was crying to beat the band. Oh, she was hurt.

"You don't believe nothing I tell you," she said in one of those pouty little girl whines.

But I made her go to her room—and she never threw another tantrum.

Part Two

Grade School and Middle School

Chapter Eight
Instilling Faith and Values

*Teach your children faith, values, and
a love for God by making church part of
their lives from an early age.*

Faith and family have been constant priorities for as long
as Ambrose and Freda Robinson can remember.

Freda's father was a Baptist deacon who died as he was pre-
viewing a Sunday school lesson. Ambrose's father has chaired
the trustee board and faithfully attended the same church for
more than fifty years. Ambrose's sister is a minister of music
who plays at churches throughout Arkansas. Ambrose and
Freda met in church.

Freda, David, Chuck, and Kimberly Robinson are all devout,
born-again Christians. Ambrose is less active, but still believes
faith is important for both individuals and families. All believe
Christianity is more than making an appearance in church for
an hour every Sunday. It's a way of life, a way to instill morals and
ethics and values in children. The Robinsons believe in God first
and foremost, a philosophy they embraced from Day One.

FREDA I won't force my beliefs on anyone, but this is what
worked for us: The most important thing was to teach our
children that Jesus Christ is everything to us. He is the center of
our lives, our family. He is our thermostat. We are merely ther-
mometers. He controls everything. He created us. Once that's

established, then morals and ethics can be instilled. But first and foremost we must know who's in charge of the entire creation.

My children were raised up in church since the day they were born. I didn't send them to church; they went with me. I think that's important. The babies were in the nursery, but as soon as they were old enough—about two or three—they began to sit in church. There were times they still played in the nursery, but by the time they were four years old, they were sitting in church beside me. If they misbehaved, I'd correct them. They were taught to give homage to the service.

You need to mold your child at an early age. It tends to sink in better than when they're older. It's like the difference between adopting a baby who's a month old versus a child who's five years old. There are certain values in that five-year-old that you're never going to change. But if I take that same child at a month old, he's like a little puppy, and I can train him better. When I got a puppy once, I told the lady at the kennel, "I don't want an old dog. I want one I can teach." It's like the sign that says, "It's easier to teach a young dog old tricks than to teach an old dog new tricks." That makes a lot of sense for children, too. You have to train them. Church helps prepare them for preschool and school. If they can't sit through a service of an hour or two, how can they sit through kindergarten?

I'm a firm believer children learn what they live. I love the Lord, but I cannot force my children to love him. I can only lead them to him. If I'm an example of anything I try to instill, they'll see that in me, and they'll ask themselves, "Do I want to be like that?"

AMBROSE When I was a child, my parents took me to church more than I wanted to go. Sunday school would start at 9:30 A.M., and services would run from 11 A.M. until almost 2 P.M. We'd go home to eat, then be back for the 4 P.M. service and then Bible study at 7 P.M. Then on Wednesday night we had prayer meetings and on Thursday nights we had choir rehearsal. We'd have choir practice for two hours, plus occasional Bible study. I resented it a little, but not too much, because I stayed in the church as a teenager. I was overwhelmed with too much, so I didn't try to push church on my children the way it was pushed on me.

My wife thought it was mandatory our children went. I would say don't make it mandatory, but do make room for Christ in your life. Don't push it on your children because if you live the life yourself and they're going to church with you, it grows on them. If you start taking your child to church at five months old and you're still taking him three years later, you don't have to say, "You have to go to church" because it's already a part of his life. That's what Freda was trying to instill. I'm not saying parents *have* to take their children to church for them to grow up properly, but I'm sure it helps, because it teaches them a lot of things.

I think the children really enjoyed it and developed a real respect and love for God, because they would often mention, "Without God, this wouldn't happen." They believed there was a being more powerful than they were.

But sometimes they just went along with the program. I know this was asked many times: "Dad's not going. Why do we have to?" I couldn't answer that. I went forty to fifty percent of the time. If I had to do it again, I'd go as a whole family all the time, not just at selective times. It goes back to: You should lead by example. What's the saying? The family that prays together stays together.

FREDA I give the Lord his time because he's blessed me. I'm not a fanatic, but I believe. You can't lose with God. If you have the Lord, you have a kind of peace the person who doesn't believe in the Lord cannot understand. I take a lot of things that I would not have taken when I had less faith. Now I can look at offensive people and walk away and smile and pray for them. Before I had no patience to do that. He's my inspiration. All of us have a right to believe what we want, but if you believe God can do anything but fail, he *can* do it.

Now, some people might say I'm a nut, but I'm a happy nut. God has been good to me and my family. I've got a reason to be happy.

Chapter Nine
Stealing Candy

Teach your children to value character
and honesty even above ability.

David looked up and down the aisle at the 7-Eleven, and no one was looking except his four-year-old brother. So, as ten-year-olds are apt to do, he slid the candy bar into his clothes and escaped without notice.

Until, that is, he got home, and Chuck started hollering because he wanted part of the candy. Their dad heard the ruckus and wondered where they got the candy.

"We got it from the store," Chuck said.

"You didn't have any money to pay for it," Ambrose said.

"David took the candy," Chuck said.

That was all Ambrose needed to hear. There would be no such thing as a little mischief, a little shoplifting, in his home. He loaded both boys into his car, drove back to the store, and made David walk up to the cashier and admit he stole the candy. Other shoppers—neighbors, friends—listened in. Nervous, embarrassed, and in tears, David confessed and apologized.

The cashier said, "Well, you can have it since you were honest enough to tell me."

The father said, "No, he cannot have it. It is not his candy."

Then he took the boys home and spanked them both with his belt, David for the crime and Chuck for going along with it.

That would be the first and last time any Robinson took what didn't belong to him.

AMBROSE I never had any problems with either of them ever stealing anything again. That's the worst they ever broke the law.

It made a big impression, a *real* big impression. The point is, when parents see something that doesn't belong to their kids, they should question it, and some of them don't.

FREDA You need to make a statement. I was so glad when Ambrose made them take back that piece of candy. It scared me; I didn't know David would have the nerve to take something out of that store. They needed to realize they'd be embarrassed, they'd be exposed. We were not going to hide it.

You can't say, "This kid won't do it because he lives on this side of town." We lived in a middle-class neighborhood. They will do it in any neighborhood until they learn it is not acceptable.

Honesty and character are the values we taught our children. Many people have ability, but they have no character. An upstanding character is something you work at; it's how you live your life, it's how you act, it's your very being. You determine what your character is. Just because you have money doesn't mean you have class. You can line up ten millionaires and maybe five of them will have class. Class is something you earn, something you exhibit, something special. Anybody can have ability. It's how you choose to use your ability that shows what kind of character you have.

AMBROSE Honesty is a big deal with me because of what I did as a child. I took things that didn't belong to me, and I broke into people's houses. That might be one of the reasons I was thrown out of college; they suspected me of breaking into some lockers. They were right, but they couldn't prove it. I never got arrested, but I did get caught once. I forged a neighbor lady's check, and my parents, being the fine and upstanding citizens they were in the community, talked to her and convinced her not to prosecute. I had forged her check to buy a Ping-Pong table, and when it came, I had it delivered to me. I was lucky. Not long after that, there was a big fire at the reform school where I would have been sent and eighty-five boys were killed.

I knew what I had done was wrong, and I did not want my children to be like that. I could spot certain things, and I just didn't accept lying and stealing. I would not take my children to the movies and lie about their ages just to get a cheaper ticket, because then they learn it's okay to lie. Even today, I cannot stand lying and cheating—even if I just see a person cheating himself on the golf course, I get upset. It's one thing to ask, "Can I roll this ball out of here a little?" but I have a problem when he tries to do it when you're not looking, when he loses his ball in the woods and suddenly "finds" it on the fairway. A lot of business gets done on the golf course, and so I do not want to do business with people who cheat me or themselves on the course. I figure if they cheat on the course, they might cheat me in business.

Chapter Ten

Learning from Mistakes and Failures

Don't put on a facade. Show your children you're a real person, that you make mistakes, but that you try to learn from them.

Good judgment comes from experience. Experience comes from bad judgment.

Ambrose saw this sign, saved it, and produced a second version on his computer. He has posted both in his offices for the past decade.

It's a lesson both adults and children can live by, because we can all learn from our failures and those of others. Mistakes can be powerful teachers. Ample evidence exists both in business and in family. Business consultant Ken Blanchard says you can take two approaches to failure: You can let the defeat define you or you can approach it with a sense of wonder, as in, why did this happen? What can I learn?

Marian Wright Edelman, founder and president of the Children's Defense Fund, calls this Rule Five of her Twenty-Five Lessons For Life: "Don't be afraid of taking risks or of being criticized. If you don't want to be criticized, don't say anything, don't do anything or be anything. Don't be afraid of failing." And Barbara Proctor advises, "Take risks. You can't fall off the bottom."

Sometimes a bad example is the best example—or at least a powerful example of what not to do . . . as long as your children are old enough to reason and draw conclusions on their own. Drinking and smoking are dangerous examples because they tend to be passed down from generation to generation, but if youngsters see how much harm the addictions cause their family, they can become staunch opponents.

AMBROSE People will say, "Well, you did it." My children said that to me about my drinking and smoking once. It took me aback, but it was the truth. They didn't like the smell of my cigarettes; I can't stand it myself sometimes. I never got drunk, but I can understand that my drinking might have bothered them. The best thing is to live what you preach. But no one is infallible. No one will be perfect all the time. I wasn't always the best example for my children.

DAVID I was never, *ever* tempted in the least to use drugs or alcohol. I saw what it did to other people, and I didn't want that to happen to me. I sure didn't want to drink when I was down, because I knew it would only make things worse. Another reason I didn't drink is that when I was growing up, my dad drank a lot of beer. I had to crush the cans and take them to be recycled. I didn't like that job. I didn't like the smell. So it didn't appeal to me to drink. I saw the effects of beer on my father's attitude, and I didn't like it. I didn't want my judgment affected, and I didn't want to be depressed because of drinking. Another thing that affected me was my dad's smoking. When we went on long trips in the car, I got sick from smelling all the smoke from his cigarettes. I've never hung out with people who drank or did drugs. I was focused on playing sports. Of course,

I heard and read about athletes who got in trouble, but I had developed such an aversion to drinking, drugs, and smoking, these things didn't attract me at all.

FREDA We let the children know we made plenty of mistakes. We let them know we were far from perfect. We knew when they were heading down the wrong road, because we'd been down that road. Ambrose did so many bad things as a teen. He thought he was so slick, more clever than everybody else, and he was a bad egg, a little terror. When he became a parent, he was determined his children would not go in that direction. If he saw them doing any little thing that might lead downhill, he'd correct them.

Children can appreciate it when we make mistakes. Then they don't feel like they have to be perfect; they know they can be themselves and still be loved. When we let our children see our imperfections, they don't feel they have to live up to impossible standards. Parents get tired, they get frustrated, and kids can see that. They know when you're being artificial. They like to see you downright upset. Then they can say, "She's just like me." I believe in being as normal as possible.

I'll give you a prime example of this. Certain of our relatives never sent Christmas gifts to our children when they were small. I'd buy gifts and hide them in the closet and put the relatives' names on them, so my children thought they hadn't been forgotten. One year my daughter said, "Ma, don't buy presents and put someone else's name on them. We saw the presents in the closet, and then we saw them under the Christmas tree with their names on them, and we know they didn't buy them. We'd just prefer you not do that."

We were trying to project the perfect family. It doesn't work, because children see through it. I was telling a lie, living a lie, and they told me that. When you're being polite all the time, they know you're lying. They think, "She can't feel positive all the time unless she's inhuman. She has to have feelings, same as I have feelings."

59

Children need to know what's real in life, need to know, "My mother's not putting on a facade. She's for real. I know her heart." When David was talking to Ed Bradley on *60 Minutes*, he said, "I trust my mother because her heart is good." That moved me because no one forced him to say it.

AMBROSE We tried to give our children direction, and we allowed them to make mistakes by not trying to solve all of their problems. If they asked, we would help, often by making several suggestions and letting them choose what was best. We tried to show them the consequences of their actions. We'd say, "This is what you want to do. These are a few ways to do it. What do you think is the best way?" The lesson was, think before you act, and it might save you embarrassment.

Learning from failure goes along with showing good judgment and taking responsibility and accepting the consequences of your actions. One of the big problems in the world today is adults don't want to take responsibility for their actions.

DAVID Failure doesn't get enough credit. It teaches us humility, perseverance, and the value of hard work. When you fail, you can learn from your mistakes and then move on.

God gives you challenges in your life for a reason. He's not trying to hurt you or punish you. He's giving you those challenges so you'll grow up and mature.

Chapter Eleven
Responsibility Breeds Confidence

*Give your children chores, show them
how to do them and show confidence they
can do them, and they will develop responsibility, self-confidence, and self-worth.*

Chuck Robinson was mowing his daddy's lawn when he
wasn't even tall enough to see over the mower's handle. And he
wasn't alone; by grade school, all the Robinson children had
their own chores. Detailed instructions were posted daily on
the refrigerator or the bulletin board. David and Chuck often
cooked, Kimberly washed dishes, and all took turns vacuum-
ing, scrubbing, and tidying up, not only their bedrooms but the
whole house. The boys mowed the lawn, trimmed the shrubs,
took out the garbage, cleaned the garage, washed the car, split
firewood, and hauled it inside.

They held outside jobs, as well. David delivered newspapers and sometimes convinced his brother to help. Kimberly
baby-sat her brothers and neighbors, and when she got older
and started working other jobs, David took over many of her
baby-sitting clients. When he was about thirteen, Chuck
started his own landscaping business, mowing all the yards of
homes for sale by a local realtor.

The chores came partly out of necessity: More often than
not, both parents worked, and often, Ambrose was working out

of town. Two years older than David and eight years older than Chuck, Kimberly became more than just the big sister. "Because my father was overseas a lot and my mother was working, I felt I had to step up. When she'd leave us in the house, I'd be the one in charge," Kimberly says. Adds Ambrose: "She was like the mother when Mother wasn't around."

But the chores had a deeper purpose, too: They taught life-long lessons in self-sufficiency and responsibility. The parents added praise and monetary rewards for these little accomplishments, and the children developed the confidence to handle much bigger projects.

Ambrose and Freda gave their children room to grow and explore, but forced them to pay the consequences if they abused their freedom. "We always knew the difference between right and wrong," David says. "We had responsibilities, but we had freedom, too. For that reason, I never felt any desire to break loose." Chuck concurs: "They gave us a great deal of freedom which developed an independent spirit in us when it came time to live on our own."

AMBROSE I didn't want my children to have idle minds. Idle minds are the devil's workshop. And so, because both of us worked, we didn't always have time to do the chores ourselves, and I'd always give the children things to keep them busy and out of trouble. I'd tell them they either had to do their studies or I'd find another chore. It was easier to study than to rake the yard. But responsibility is much more than doing chores or being obedient. It means caring about how your actions make other people feel and understanding why rules are important.

Some people say I pushed them too fast. I remember when we built the deck at the back of our house. I poured the foundations, got the lumber, and measured everything, then grabbed a beer and watched my two teenage boys do the rest. They did an excellent job. Some of our friends said, "You shouldn't do that," but those same people tell me they wish they had taught their children that responsibility earlier, because their children didn't turn out so well.

FREDA Ambrose would build TVs himself. He would buy David small electronic kits and he would work on the big one. Sometimes he'd work on the small kit with David to help him learn. David would read the directions, and he knew the difference between a transistor, a diode, and a capacitor when he was still in elementary school.

AMBROSE How else do you teach a child what a tool is? If a child doesn't know what a pair of needle-nose pliers are for . . . well, children need to learn household basics for proficiency in selecting the right tool for a job, changing a plug on a broken lamp, or helping Dad change the oil or tune the car.

I showed my children how to operate the TV and stereo. They were going to play with it anyway, so why not show them the right way and avoid a repair bill? All my children learned to become self-sufficient at an early age.

FREDA When we were in Key West, Ambrose would take our car to a mechanic who taught Ambrose how to fix it himself. He'd say, "Look, you don't have to bring it back to me. When this happens, do this," and he'd show Ambrose exactly how to fix whatever it was. When we left there, Ambrose knew how to fix his own cars. My boys could change their own oil. Kim can change her oil. She has an oil pan and everything she needs to change the oil and filter. Kim can go and buy a piece of furniture or an exercise machine and assemble it.

A lot of people would say, "I can't do that." Oh, yes, you can.

Chapter Twelve

Sibling Rivalry and Competition

*Turn the natural sibling rivalries into
positive competitions.*

FREDA You cannot appreciate the Robinsons until you see them in action at the bowling alley. We get so crazy, it's like a circus. All the people in the bowling alley will stop bowling and stand behind us and watch and start cheering. There will be droves of people standing behind us. The security guard will have to keep them back. We were drawing crowds even before David became famous. You don't have to be Captain Kangaroo to get attention. We don't try to get attention; we're just having fun.

There's a lot of trash talking, and my nephew Mitch will tell you that Ambrose is the worst. Ambrose tries to distract you. He'll say something like, "Man, you can't bowl! Put up or shut up!" I remember one time he got on David when everybody was beating him. David had to roll five strikes in a row to win—and he did!

David and his daddy, my gosh, you'd think they were the two worst enemies. They talk bad about each other and burn each other up. They're always telling each other, "You know you don't like to pay up!" People probably think David is too nice to talk trash, but he does, whether it's bowling or golfing. Or, as Mitch puts it: "Big trash talker, biiiiggggg trash talker."

64

And then there's Ambrose, acting as if he's the baddest thing out there. But if he loses, he always acts as if his back is out.

Ambrose saunters out there like the Pink Panther, like he's going to kill everybody, and then he throws the ball, and turns around and kicks his leg in the air and goes "Woooo." And then David throws the ball so hard, it feels like the whole bowling alley is going to shatter. It's so wild. Mitch walks down the lane as if he's going to church. I go up there, lay my ball down and go back to my seat, but I don't lay down for them. I scare them a little because they know I can bowl when I put my mind to it.

Ambrose, Mitch, David, and I bowl together, and sometimes David's wife Valerie joins in. Chuck and Kim will, too, if they're in town. They're at each other's throats. It can be a lot of fun.

AMBROSE I carry a 194, 195 average and David carries a 198, and we have a heckuva time at the bowling alley. David is a twelve handicap and I'm a fourteen, and we have a heckuva time on the golf course. Chuck comes into town and it really gets heated up. Kim comes into town and heats it up even more. And then Mitch joins us and we have a ball.

A lot of these competitive juices sprang from sibling rivalry when they were little. They always thought they could out-do the other. I tried to instill that competitive spirit early on. One of the ways I did it was with my own competitiveness. I can take you back to high school, when I was the only boy in typing class and I was trying to be number one and ended up number two. I was typing ninety-six words a minute and this girl, I'll never forget her name—Gloria Ray—was typing ninety-nine words a minute, and I never could catch her.

I was very competitive in baseball and bowling. When I became a father, I'd take my children to the city leagues or the bowling alley, or we'd go hit some golf balls, or go play football or baseball in the backyard. We'd play board games like Monopoly and try to beat each other. We'd holler that somebody had to be cheating. Sometimes, one of us would quit before the game ended, just to avoid losing.

FREDA You hear a lot about sibling rivalry, but it's not all bad. It keeps siblings from lagging behind each other. It makes them more competitive with others.

Rivalry between siblings is normal and starts at a very young age. You have a baby on your lap, and the other one wants to climb up. Siblings without rivalry? That's almost impossible. When there's more than one child, you have to divide your time among them, and one will always fall short of the others. So you do it based on individual needs. If one's sick or has a problem or simply isn't as secure, he needs more attention.

Sibling rivalry can be channeled in a positive direction. My family is so competitive, nobody wants to lose, and they go at it like there's money involved. One emulating something the other is doing, as long as it's positive, is great for them. When David was in college and well known, reporters would ask Chuck, "Are you planning to go to the Academy like your brother?" But he didn't want to be in David's shadow. He would always say, "No, I'll never go to the Academy." And look where he ended up. He found the Academy wasn't all bad. Sibling rivalry in our family has been there from Day One until now, but I don't recall it ever being a problem.

AMBROSE As children they'd fuss and fight among themselves, as any siblings do, but not a lot. They'd always stick up for each other if an outsider picked on one. And as they've grown older, they've grown closer. Everybody is real tight now. That doesn't happen in some families. It really makes me feel good.

Chapter Thirteen
Visions and Goals

─────────

*Parents should have a vision of what
their children can become, and help them
set goals and work toward them.*

Talk to any of the Robinsons very long and you'll hear the word *vision*—and they're not talking about Elton John's eyeglass collection. They say parents must have an overriding vision that will give each child a direction and a purpose. That focus will help guide the child, and setting goals and working toward them along the way will help the child achieve that vision as well as other accomplishments.

The vision should be flexible, geared more toward generalities such as being a good student and good person rather than toward specifics such as being a lawyer and Harvard grad.

AMBROSE I believe in setting goals and working systematically toward them. I didn't stress short-term goals as much as I did long-term goals such as education. If you ask David about goals, he'll remember I used to tell him, "If you ever meet your goal and stop there, you've failed, because you've stopped trying." For instance, if my goal is to get to college and when I get there, I don't graduate, I've failed to set my goals high enough. So you need progressive goals, goals that build on each other.

CHUCK They did a great job instilling in us their expectations, which became our expectations. They had to be *our* expectations if we wanted to do anything else. In our house it was not okay to get a D. We knew we better bring home good grades or else.

Most parents just want children who don't end up on drugs. That was never even an option for us. Our only options were to do well in school and graduate from college. We had no choice. There was no question in our minds whether we'd go to college or not. We were going to go.

Nowadays, a lot of parents let their children dictate to them what's going to happen in their lives. They say, "No, Ma, I don't want to play football." Or "No, Ma, I just don't like English." But my parents *never* let us dictate to them what we were going to do. They *always* let us know what the standards were. If we met them, great, and if we didn't, we paid the consequences. There was no better way to grow up.

FREDA Our goal was that all our children would go to college. It wasn't a command, but it was understood, almost an automatic. We were always saying they should do well in school so they could get a college scholarship, because we didn't have a lot of money, and we wanted them to go to a good school.

It's good to set goals for even little things. Kim made a dollar an hour baby-sitting, but she saved that little bit of money until she reached a certain goal. She had special tastes, and she worked to get what she wanted. For instance, the only jeans she would buy were Gloria Vanderbilt. Then she wanted a moped. Her father said he wouldn't buy it because it was dangerous, but she was determined to have it, and she saved $600 to buy it. That's a lot of hours baby-sitting.

Once I told David's godmother I thought Kim was being wasteful. She said, "You have good children. Kim worked hard to save this money. She has a right to nice things if she wants them. Look at it this way: If she's accustomed to having nice things, she'll always work hard to buy them." I thought about it, and it made sense. Always work hard for the best.

Chapter Fourteen

Pushing Education

*Prod and motivate your children to
achieve their full academic potential.*

Learning came early and easily for David Robinson. He
read at age three, played the piano at five, and knew his lessons
so well by second grade, he'd finish the work ahead of everyone
else and start talking and bothering the other children. The
teacher and principal wanted to skip him ahead to third grade,
but his parents said no, to just keep giving him more advanced
work until he could do no more. A year later, David joined the
brand new gifted-child program in Virginia Beach, and continued to excel even among the city's smartest students. They
were allowed to take courses at a magnet school one day a
week, and when they reached sixth or seventh grade, they took
night courses at the local junior college in subjects such as
speed reading, algebra, and advanced math.

A math whiz by the third grade, David would go to the grocery store with his mom and he'd figure the costs per ounce and
total tab, and if she were short of cash, he'd tell her what she
needed to put back. She called him her "human calculator."

By junior high, his math teacher would drive to the Robinson house, drop off all the students' tests, and let David grade
them. Once, the instructor forgot to leave the master sheet.
When David called to tell him, the teacher simply said, "You

don't need the master sheet. You already know the answers."
And he did.

In eighth grade, David brought home a report card that
would make most parents proud: an A, two B's, and a C.

He got grounded for six weeks.

"It was a subject he normally did well in, and all of a sudden he had a C," Ambrose recalls. "That told me he wasn't
studying or something was wrong. Maybe he was trying to get
back at us, but I fixed him. That's how I instilled that you-
better-be-serious nature."

Until he boosted that C the next time grades came out, he
could not leave his house or yard to play with his friends after
school.

"For a kid, that's a long restriction," David says, the lesson
still with him nearly twenty years later. "But they knew I wasn't
supposed to be getting a C. Whether I was having a problem
with the teacher or whether I decided I wasn't going to do the
work, it was unacceptable. There was no reason for me to ever
get a C. Seldom did I see other parents take drastic measures
like that."

But the Robinsons didn't just encourage best efforts when
it came to education, they demanded them. Even when Chuck
got almost straight A's in high school, they always asked if he
could have done more.

"They were tougher than all my friends' parents," Chuck
says. "We had our own standards. I always hung out with the
most popular people in school. We'd be sitting around when we
got report cards and one guy would say, 'Oh, my mom is going
to kill me because I got a D.' The next guy would say, 'I failed
English.' I'd never tell them I had a 3.8 and I'd get in trouble if
I'd gotten a C. My friends didn't apply themselves. I did,
because I knew what standards I had to meet. So I attribute my
education to my parents."

Is it any wonder all their children got good grades? That
David scored 1320 out of 1600 on the SATs? That the two boys
graduated from the prestigious and demanding Naval Acad-

emy? That the only girl earned an MBA and is working on her doctorate?

DAVID I was lazy when it came to studying. Lazy probably doesn't even begin to describe it. I was a gifted learner, and when things come easily to you, if your personality isn't that get-up-and-go type, it's easy to be lazy. I really had to be pushed to achieve.

My parents were stricter than most. They got much more upset about grades and results than most parents. I always felt their standards were way too high, so if I did enough to get by their standards, that was way more than most kids.

But when I got to the Naval Academy, doing just enough to get by wasn't enough. Everybody was tops in their class, incredibly smart, and so I was pushed to a higher level, and I began to understand why my parents had always expected so much. When you've always excelled, you think there can't be that many people smarter than you. Then you get to an environment like the Naval Academy, and you're pushed even more. It was the best thing that could have happened to me.

FREDA I pushed David hard, and I'll tell you why: Most parents know their children's capabilities. David was a little laid back, but I knew he could learn anything he wanted to. I always saw success in him. I pictured him as a research scientist, but I always wanted him to be a neurosurgeon.

Those who are unusually quick to conquer material tend to be more laid back about it and ask, "Why work myself to death?" This is what bothered me about David: He had the ability to retain all this material, but he was lax, with a matter-of-fact attitude. A lot of times he got good grades, but didn't give his best. I have no patience for people who do just enough to get by. I told all of them if they made an A and could have made an A-plus, they might as well have made an F, because they hadn't given their all. Maybe at times I was a little too hard, but I don't think so.

71

All of them needed to be prodded a little. Kim had to study harder than the boys, but she applied herself more than they did. Her grades weren't as great, but she always gave it her best shot. Chuck was the most laid back of all of them. He was today's student: "I'm doing what you asked. I'm going to school and I'm no dummy. What more do you want?"

We stressed that they do their best, but even though you can make them sit down and study, you can't control how much attention and interest they have in the subject.

AMBROSE You encourage your children to do those things you think are necessary for them to survive in life. But you can cross the line and push too hard if you force them to do something they really don't want to do without explaining the benefits. If you can help them see the benefits, whether or not they want to do something, that's great.

Chapter Fifteen

Help Your Children Learn

Take a proactive role in your children's education: Establish a study regimen, check on homework, and promote curiosity.

Like most families, the Robinsons didn't have all kinds of money to send their children to exclusive private schools. But they did try to live in the best school district they could afford. And they did stress education on a daily basis. They didn't just mouth the words, they meant them. They demanded their children study. They developed a regular homework routine and reviewed assignments.

They didn't limit learning to the classroom. They coached curiosity. They sparked intelligence. They read to their children and encouraged them to read. They bought flashcards and quizzed them. They bought educational toys and electronic kits and allowed the children to help put them together. They watched TV shows the children could learn from, such as *Jeopardy* and *Name That Tune*. They encouraged the children to help as they worked around the house and car, and they explained what they were doing, how to do it, why to do it.

FREDA The children had a regular routine. They'd be tired and hungry when they came home from school, so I'd let them eat and take a little rest period, and then do their homework. They couldn't go anywhere until they finished their homework. If they didn't bring something home, we gave them something to do. Most days they had homework, but if they didn't, we figured they needed to study anyway. If they came home two or three days in a row and said they didn't have homework in a certain subject, we'd make them read from a book on that subject.

I'd look over the homework before they did it. If I thought they could master it, I'd leave them alone to do it. They might need a little help, but I wanted them to do it. Even if I helped them, I'd let them make the final decision on a problem. I might explain and guide, but I would not do the work for them or teach them again. I was there to make sure they followed the instructions and completed the work.

They'd learn words playing Scrabble and learn about records from the Guiness Book of World Records. Most of the toys we bought promoted learning, and we played a lot of games with them. Ambrose would tell them, "You have more opportunities than I had, and we want you to build on that, to take advantage of the opportunities."

We'd do all kinds of things to motivate them when they didn't show interest. I'd try to get extra books for them to read that were similar to those in a certain class. I'd spend more time with them on their homework. If David knew his homework, we'd diversify. We'd give him more work on a higher level. It would keep him occupied, so he wouldn't disturb the other children. He would finish his work, no matter what you gave him. A lot of times David would do his homework before he got home. He could do it in a heartbeat.

AMBROSE We didn't have all these Nintendo games back then, and my children never watched that much TV, so I never had to restrict it. As long as they got their homework done, I didn't have a problem with them watching TV.

FREDA I never had much trouble getting the children to finish their work. I just had to make sure they got started.

Before they could go out and play or do anything else, they had to show their work to their daddy, and they didn't want to show him something that wasn't finished.

They didn't want to upset their daddy. Ambrose was a disciplinarian. I was cautious of being too much of a disciplinarian because my father had been one. So I tried to soften up Ambrose. I wanted them to do the homework, too, but my methods varied. I would deny them something they wanted, some place they wanted to go, take away their favorites. Ambrose would sometimes deny *and* punish. He says if he could do it all over, he would go a little easier, but I would change very few things. I'm glad Ambrose was hard on them. Never mind the method. It worked.

AMBROSE I always considered myself a jack of all trades, and probably a master of none, so there was nothing I wouldn't try to tackle. A lot of times, David would be there watching. That's where a lot of his curiosity came from. I loved to tear something apart to see how it worked, why it didn't work, and to try to fix it. A lot of the wide range of interests David has now probably came from me. I would buy something that would cost $400 or $500—a lot of money in those days—and I'd work or play with it for a while and then I'd put it aside and go to something else. After a while, it didn't hold my interest anymore. It wasn't challenging enough. David is the same way today. He'll buy a computer and play with it for a while, get bored and buy another one. Of course, he probably can afford more expensive toys now than I could then.

Chapter Sixteen

Expose and Enlighten

Don't insulate your children in a little corner of the world. Expose them to different places and peoples.

Like most military families, the Robinsons could have used magic furniture, the kind that jumps into the moving boxes and unpacks itself when it's time to move again. From the time Kimberly was born in 1963, they lived in Newport, Rhode Island (1962–1964), Key West, Florida (1964–1966), Newport again (1966), Key West again (1967–1969), Portsmouth, New Hampshire (1969), Norfolk, Virginia (1970–1973), and Virginia Beach, Virginia (1973–1982).

Even after Ambrose retired from the Navy in 1981, they moved again. He took a government consulting job just outside Washington D.C., and after commuting 185 miles each way for a year, he bought a house in Woodbridge, Virginia, twenty-five miles south of D.C. The family lived there until Ambrose and Freda joined David in San Antonio in 1989 and Chuck went away to the Naval Academy. Chuck has been stationed in Biloxi, Mississippi, since 1993. Kimberly still lives in the Woodbridge house.

Coping with all these changing environments, losing old friends and making new ones, adjusting to new schools—all this could have been rough on the children. But Ambrose and

Freda always emphasized the positives, and showed the children how traveling could also be enlightening. It was just one way they exposed them to this multi-colored world of ours.

FREDA When we went to Korea to watch David play in the 1988 Olympics, we could have stayed in a hotel, but we thought we'd learn more by staying with a family. We did and they were super to us. They took us to the park, drove us almost to the North Korean line, showed us the first schoolhouse in Korea. It was an education, but not as much for the history as for what we learned about the people. We got to see their culture, got to eat their food, got to see the way they lived and worked.

Traveling is a way to expose children to new things. We tried to expose our children to everything we could. We always wanted them to be well-rounded, to have a little knowledge of all subjects. You don't have to excel in everything, but you should at least be able to talk about most things. Even in sports. A lot of people have said, "Why did you let David play so many sports? Why didn't you have him just focus on one or two?" To me, that's like taking him to the movies and never to a play, an opera, or anything else.

Moving is educational. You learn to make friends. Ambrose and I have never had problems communicating with people, and the children saw that and never had a problem with it, either. They kept in touch with their old friends, but they also made new friends. We would be moving into a new house, and they would already have met the kids next door. We taught our children to be open and receptive to change.

We tried to buy in the best neighborhoods we could afford. But when we did that, we didn't find a lot of blacks, and we knew it was important to expose our children to their own people. So I still took them to black neighborhoods; I wanted them to understand their identity. It's not teaching them to be for somebody or against somebody; it's teaching them to know their heritage.

Children need to be exposed to different environments. Then you won't see them staring at a person of another race as if that person were an alien. I can walk into a grocery store in certain neighborhoods and when the children stare at me, I know they haven't seen many black women; they've been shielded. It was probably done ignorantly or unconsciously. If I've got to take my children to the circus to show them that there are black people, red people, Chinese people, Filipino people, and Mexican people in the world, I'll do it.

We must mold our children at an early age, before they learn about segregation and prejudice. For instance, if you let ten different nationalities run around a park, the young children will all play together, whereas the adults will stand off in their own little huddles. We need to quit teaching our children all these myths about race and instead show them that we're all human beings. I believe a lot of our race problems could be solved by just mingling and getting to know other people.

Chapter Seventeen
Read and Grow

Promote reading.

His mom finally had a Saturday off, and little David wasted no time pouncing. He was a fifth-grade science-fiction junkie, and Freda had promised to buy him a fix.

So off they went to the bookstore, and David quickly found the exact book he wanted—along with all the other books in the series.

"Geeeee!" he exclaimed. "All five right here! Mom, can you buy them all?"

"No," Freda said. "You said you wanted one book, and I've only got seven dollars with me."

"Mom," he replied, "don't you have a charge card? Put it on that!"

"He's right," David's godmother chimed in. "Put it on your charge card. You put everything else you want on it. If my kids would read like David, I would buy the whole library and bring it home."

Freda was outnumbered. Her husband felt the same way: If a child wants a book, buy it. You can spoil children with too many toys, but you can never spoil them with too many books. What better way is there to learn?

Of all the grade-school subjects, reading might be the most important. It's not just a matter of vocabulary and comprehension. Reading equips you so that you can learn about every

79

other subject. It helps you communicate, helps you become a learned child and adult. A child who doesn't read well, who doesn't read often, is like an athlete who cannot run fast: He's at a severe disadvantage at just about everything he tries.

So the Robinsons instilled the love of reading early. They bought fun books like Dr. Seuss and various science-fiction series. They bought educational books. They bought magazines like Highlights For Children. They taught their children how to use the library.

What if you do all this and your children still don't like to read? Try this tip from child advocate Marian Wright Edelman: She says the only time her dad didn't give her a chore was when she was reading—so she read a lot.

AMBROSE I'd always find something to keep the children busy. If they didn't have anything else to do, I'd tell them to pick up the dictionary. What better way to find out things? I did it as a child, and I did it a lot in the Navy; you don't have that much else to do in your free time when you're on a ship out at sea. It helped make me the best Scrabble player around.

FREDA If my children came across a word they didn't know, they'd say, "Mom, what does this mean?" and I'd say, "Get the dictionary" because I knew they'd remember it better if they looked it up. Kim and Chuck liked to read, but David *loved* to read. The more David read, the more he loved it. When everybody else was out playing sports, David would be sitting in the back of a classroom reading a book. The other kids looked at him like he was a reading nerd, a bookworm.

AMBROSE I'd make them go to bed at a certain time every night. Some nights I'd go check on David—and he'd be under the cover with a flashlight reading a book. Well, he was supposed to be asleep because he had to get up at 5:30 or 6 o'clock to catch the bus to go to school. But it's hard to be upset when a child wants to read more.

FREDA If the power went out, and I needed the flashlight, I always knew where to find it—in David's room.

Chapter Eighteen

Mr. Rogers' and Mr. Robinson's Neighborhoods

Don't make music mandatory, but encourage it because it can bring lifelong enjoyment.

Remember the series of Mr. Robinson's Neighborhood commercials that were takeoffs on *Mr. Rogers' Neighborhood*?

It turns out, David Robinson and Fred Rogers have more in common than just a similar surname and a calm demeanor.

Both have a love for the piano that goes back to early childhood. It's a good way for people of all ages to relieve stress. Fred Rogers says when he was angry as a child, he'd go to the piano and "could cry through the ends of my fingers or laugh through the ends of my fingers. It was a great gift. Music was a way of expressing feelings." Likewise, Ambrose Robinson spent countless adult hours unwinding on the piano, releasing the tension from his daily commute. Even as a toddler, David would listen to his dad, then climb up and bang away on the keys. But quickly, he picked up the notes, and gradually, he put them together and played by ear. His father taught him how to play, and how to read music, and surprisingly, one of the first pieces he played was Beethoven's "Moonlight Sonata." Though David has taken only a few formal lessons, Ambrose says David now plays much better than he does, and music might even be his favorite hobby. He has had formal saxophone lessons, and he can play the alto, tenor, and soprano sax. He plays guitar a little, and he takes portable keyboards on virtually every Spurs road trip. He plays classical and jazz and pop music. He composes his own songs. He can hear a song and play it by ear. He has jammed with such sax stars as Grover Washington and Branford Marsalis.

One of those Nike commercials even features a duel with a great pianist.

"Today, we have a special visitor," David says in his softest Mr. Rogers voice. "It's Rudolf Firkusny. He's going to play classical piano with Mr. Robinson. Bo may know Diddley. But Mr. Robinson knows Beethoven!"

They start playing, but it's obvious Robinson can't keep up.

"Gee, Mr. Firkusny is better at the piano," Robinson says, his voice soft, his eyes dazed. But then he gives his meanest scowl, and takes the grand old man to a basketball court, and starts flying by him, jamming over him, and he says, "But Mr. Robinson can really cream him at basketball!"

It's a funny little spot that few other athletes could have shot.

AMBROSE Growing up, I took piano lessons for about ten years and played in church as a teenager. My whole family was musically inclined. My mother played for years and years, my sister has a masters in music, and my dad sings in the choir.

FREDA Ambrose used to play for me when we were dating. When his mother would come and visit us before she passed, she'd play for us. When she'd start singing, she had such a beautiful voice, I'd stop whatever I was doing to listen. Music can bring so much joy and pleasure. We tried to interest all the children in music, but David was the only one who pursued it to any degree.

AMBROSE David became interested because he heard me playing, but I never pushed it. I was forced to take music, and I didn't want to force it on my children. David wanted to learn how.

82

Kim and Chuck were never interested, and I never worried about it. It's not essential for all children. Chuck is just starting to play the keyboards now, and he wishes he had learned earlier.

I play piano now because it relaxes me. I used to play just about every day after I retired from the Navy and went to work in Crystal City. I'd spend an hour and a half or two hours commuting twenty-five miles home to Woodbridge, and then I'd sit down and play the piano and it would relax me, unwind me. I love classical music, and I still use it as background music at home and at work. David and I both like jazz, as well.

FREDA David has enjoyed playing with Grover Washington and Branford Marsalis, but he can't play like they play. Branford says David should stick to basketball.

Chapter Nineteen

Sports Lessons

Teach your children a variety of sports,
but push books, not balls.

In grade school, David Robinson was more bookworm than jock, even though sports came naturally to him. He competed in just about everything and usually won. He'd run in the front door, sound an imaginary trumpet, and lay three or four first-place blue ribbons on the kitchen table for his mom to admire.

When he was nine or ten, he won the Virginia long jump competition and went to Kentucky to compete in the national finals. He fell in the finals—and still took second. And yet when his mom picked him up, he did not show her his ribbon.

"He had a long face and said, 'Mom, I didn't want to show it to you. I only won the red,'" Freda recalls. "He was second in the nation and yet disappointed. But I'm glad he was like that. It's good to set high standards for yourself.

"It may sound strange to say this, but I always thought his sport would be baseball. He seemed to have everything he needed for baseball: He could run, he could throw, and he could hit. I still remember David's community league games; he couldn't have been much more than nine years old at the time. Every time David came to bat, the people in the stand would bet on him to hit a home run. And he could do it, too, right-handed or left-handed."

When he was eleven, his father took him to a driving range and gave him his first golf lesson. It wasn't easy, because Ambrose's clubs were too big, and made for a right-hander, not a left-hander, as David is. And yet David promptly went out, and with his dad telling him which club to use and how to use it, shot about a 124 and won the tournament for his age group.

"It was amazing, it really was," Ambrose says.

Still, Ambrose only considered David a slightly above average athlete. He certainly wasn't a basketball superstar back then: He was a backup in eighth grade, and he quit in ninth grade because he played so little for the middle-school team, and he did not play again until his senior year of high school.

Chuck was a far more accomplished basketball player even though he was much shorter than his big brother, and he also excelled in track and football. Kimberly played baseball and softball in community leagues, ran track in junior high, and played tennis in high school.

Ambrose had played football and basketball and run track in high school; he thought segregation robbed him of a chance to play major-college and pro ball. Still, he was not a wannabe trying to build a robot athlete. He viewed sports as a diversion, not a career path, for his children. Neither he nor his wife pushed athletics the way they pushed academics. They did not try to make star athletes; they stressed education and career.

Ambrose did, however, spend a large portion of his time with his children—playing and teaching them to play just about every sport around. He was in his early twenties when his first two children were born; an overgrown kid who liked to play alongside his own.

AMBROSE It's a lot of fun growing up with your kids. When you're younger, you can run from first base to third with them. You can throw a football with them. Sometimes I wonder: What if I had been older? What if I weren't athletic? How would they have turned out then?

We always did a lot as a family, and when the ship was in, we would go fishing, play golf, bowl, play baseball, throw footballs, play basketball, and play tennis. I'd teach them the directions and rules and regulations of any and all sports we participated in, and then I played with them. I never pushed a sport on them, but I taught them enough about each sport that if they wanted to play, they at least knew how.

I taught bowling for a year in Virginia Beach for youngsters nine to twelve, and I loved it. I taught David to hit left- and right-handed in my backyard. I was an assistant coach in Little League baseball and in pee-wee football. The main thing I tried to teach was teamwork: working together, getting the job done, following instructions, doing what the coaches told you to do, and winning.

We didn't emphasize winning like they do today. Today, it's stressed to win at all costs. Back then, we stressed it's great to win and do the best you can to win, but if we don't, no big deal. Now, if you don't win, you may lose your coaching job—even in Little League. That's not right. It's good to teach kids how to win, but winning should not be that big a deal at this age.

We always had problems with parents. Parents want to bicker and gripe. They all want their children to play, but if you have twelve kids on a baseball team, you can't play but nine at a time. You want to put your best people out there and try to get a lead. The others probably aren't playing because they can't play that well. I don't believe you have to play everyone equally, but everyone should get some quality playing time. You always try to get each child in. Maybe it's only two or three minutes, but it's something. You still teach winning and teamwork and leadership.

We'd watch sports on television and read about them, too. I was a great sports fan and I'm still a sports nut. You ask David his favorite sport as a kid—he used to love to watch football. We followed the Miami Dolphins with Jim Kiick, Mercury Morris, and Larry Csonka, and he could still tell you about them, because he used to watch football all the time. The funny thing is, I didn't watch much of the NBA before he joined the pros because I thought the NBA was boring. I watched college basketball, but I didn't watch much pro basketball until the playoffs. Just like baseball now: I only watch during the playoffs and World Series.

We didn't shoot hoops much together until David got to college and Chuck got to middle school. I was on an archery team in high school, and David and I were good at that. We'd take a bow and arrow and target shoot in the back yard. We played a lot of Ping-Pong, too. We still do, same as we still bowl and golf together. It's good to teach these sports they can play for a lifetime. Golf, you can play until you die. Even now, David's son D.J. is only 2 1/2, but David plays catch with him and has him swinging little plastic golf clubs. I have no doubt by the time D.J. is four, I'll have him out on the course, doing some things. I'm looking forward to that. We take him out to the driving range now and let him swing.

The boys were good at gymnastics, too. We had hedges four feet high in the front yard, and they could tumble and flip right over them. David's still good at it. A year or two ago, the Spurs' coach said if David could walk on his hands to halfcourt, he'd suspend practice for the rest of the day. David walked on his hands the length of the court, and that was the end of practice. The players loved it—they'll do anything to get out of practice.

Chapter Twenty
Different Strokes

Treat your children as individuals—
because they are.

We are all different from one another, even if we are brothers, even if we are twins, and so it is a mistake to treat us all alike. It would be nice to have one set of rules that are perfectly consistent for everyone, but it doesn't work. Parents must adjust to each child based on his or her personality and how he or she responds to praise, criticism, and discipline.

FREDA You can't treat all children the same. It just doesn't work. Each child is an individual with his or her own personality. However, they all have the same basic needs, and you can be consistent in how you choose to meet those needs.

David was slick and knew how to get away with things you wouldn't see. For instance, if two children were talking in school and the teacher would tell them to stop, David would keep talking, but the other boy would be the one who got caught. Chuck would be the one caught talking. He just wouldn't leave it alone.

I've had three different children. Kim was high strung, Chuck was a show-me child, and David was more curious than show-me. David was laid back, carefree, and read a lot. Kim would cry at the drop of a pin. You didn't have to do anything to her and she'd start screaming. David's little boy is the same way. D.J. will sniff and get mad and say softly, "Go away, go away." You should be more mindful of children's feelings, but you have to be careful, because they learn very fast how to manipulate you and get away with things.

The two boys would team up on Kim. She was the oldest, but she was smaller than David. She wanted things her way. She was bossy, the boys would say. She wanted to be in charge. Maybe I put that on her, because I'd go to work and tell her she's the oldest and they had to listen to her. That's something I'd do differently now; it's not the best thing. She felt that little authority even when I was home. I'd have to stop her sometimes.

Kim was very neat, and she didn't want the boys in her room, because they'd mess it up like their rooms, typical boys' rooms that looked like a cyclone had gone through them. Kim would get so mad, she'd scream, "Ma, make Chuck get out of my room. That little brat!" She looked at Chuck as a bad egg when he was just being a typical little boy. If you try to keep a little boy out of a room, he'll keep trying to get in. Chuck would show her.

KIMBERLY Chuck used to get away with just about everything. You'd lock your bedroom door, and Chuck would pick the lock. He could take a screwdriver and get into the bedroom. Chuck thought if you wanted to keep him out, there was a reason why, and so he was determined to find a way in. Chuck managed to get away with more because my parents were tired by the time he started acting up. Chuck would say things to them that David and I wouldn't even have thought about saying.

AMBROSE You definitely have to deal with children differently, based on each one's personality. You'll start seeing the differences between them when they're young, maybe two or three, and especially by four.

I know there was favoritism, but the differences in gender, age, and activities caused some of that. When David was in high school and Chuck was in middle school, I'd go to as many of their games as I could. After David graduated from high school,

I attended a lot of Navy practices, and Chuck would go with me when he could. Kim is the one who didn't get as much of my attention. In college, she didn't play sports, and sports is what I liked. But she was hard at work trying to finish school, and she was off doing her own thing. If I had to do it again, I probably would spend more time with my daughter.

You don't even show your love to every child the same way. You'll sometimes tend to do more for one than you will another. I know the experts say you shouldn't, and I don't mean to do it blatantly. It's dangerous to show too much favoritism; you can cause a child to have a complex. But doing it a little is just human nature, and it's not all bad. The reason I say that is twofold. My brother is six years younger than me, and he was treated differently than I was. The same thing happened with my children. We get easier with each child. The younger ones get away with more.

If you've established the discipline early, you can let up a little once they know the rules. Of course, that might be why Chuck rebelled more than Kim and David. Kim and David would answer, "Yes, Daddy." Chuck would always ask why: "Why do I have to do it? What's it going to cause?" This isn't all bad, but when you want your kids to do some things, you don't want them to question everything. In retrospect, I would have been tougher with Chuck in some situations. I was a disciplinarian, but I don't think I was that tough, at least not on Chuck.

Chapter Twenty-One

Establishing Expectations and Discipline

Explain the house rules; make sure your children stick to them, and discipline them if they don't.

Chuck was in middle school when he got chastised for breaking a family rule and decided he'd had enough of the Robinson rules. He told his brother he was running away, and he started packing his clothes in a big cardboard box.

David tiptoed upstairs and whispered to his mom, "Chuck is down there packing and says he's running off. He says he'd rather be in jail than in our house, because our house is worse than Lorton."

Lorton was a nearby jail, infamous for its vicious criminals.

Freda figured Chuck had set David up, hoping big brother would tell Mom and she'd get all worried and beg him not to leave and let him bend the rules. She wasn't about to fall for it.

She waited a few minutes before she went to their bedroom and asked, calm as could be, what Chuck was doing.

Always quick to invent a story, Chuck replied, "I'm cleaning out my drawers because they're junky."

"Then what do you need this box for?" Freda asked.

"I'm laying my clothes out until I clean the drawer," Chuck said.

"Okay, Chuck," his mom said. "You want to run away? Don't waste any time, honey. Let's get this stuff out of the drawers together. I'll help you."

And she pulled six or seven drawers open and threw his clothes in the box as fast as she could.

"Let's get this out of here quick," she said. "This is good! We'll have more space in the house!"

"Noooo," Chuck said. "I don't want any help. I'm not running away! David told a story."

"How did you know David told me you were going to run off if you didn't say it?" Freda said, and Chuck was stumped for an answer. "If you want to go, it's fine," Freda went on. "But I'm not going to have you out in the cold, not eating meals. I'll take you to the nearest jail, to Lorton, and I'll leave you with the sheriff. I can't have you running the street. I'll take you down there with the other bad boys. They'll lock you up and give you three meals a day, and I won't have to worry."

Chuck's eyes grew wide. He wondered if his mom knew the sheriff, and if she were serious. But he knew she didn't usually joke about the rules, and he wasn't about to take any chances.

"Mom, I wasn't running off," he said and started putting all his stuff back in the drawers just as fast as he could.

She had not gotten upset, had not raised her voice or her hand, but she had gotten her point across very succinctly. Chuck Robinson would live by the rules as long as he lived in this house. Never again did he threaten to run away.

FREDA I didn't try to be authoritative to the point of making them timid. I told them, "Listen, some things are expected in this house. For one, you'll love and respect each other. And you'll go to school. If you don't go to school, you'll go to work. You won't sit and play and idle around. You have to stay out of trouble. There are things expected of you in life. You're doing these things to help yourself."

As a parent, you have to set up guidelines so your children will know what they are supposed to do, and then, if they ignore the guidelines, they will be disciplined. You've got to be consistent with the rules and teach them responsibility. You cannot raise a child without discipline.

That is Scripture: Spare the rod and spoil the child. I don't mean to beat a child to death. The type of discipline depends on the child. What works for one child may not work for another. Some children you can talk to, and some need a little spanking. Or you can discipline by taking something away you know is important to them. You need to get their attention.

AMBROSE I was more of a disciplinarian than Freda. But I was too dogmatic. I would change that. Some of my bossiness probably came from spending twenty years in the Navy, where the management style was to give orders and expect them to be carried out, no questions asked. I may have carried that mentality home with me. If I wouldn't let a nine-teen-year-old enlisted man talk back to me, I sure wasn't going to listen to my ten- or twelve-year-old.

One of the reasons I retired was because I was sick of teenagers coming into the Navy who didn't have respect for authority. They'd tell you where to go in a minute. They'd say, "I'm not doing that. You can't make me do that." You can't run a ship, let alone a Navy, with people like that. I'm not looking for blind obedience, but I'm looking for respect for authority. If you're in a war and you don't fire the missile when I tell you, we could all be killed. I didn't need that aggravation.

The more I think about it now, just the nature of being a Navy supervisor and dealing with youngsters—often teenagers—caused a lot of my dogmatism at home.

CHUCK At times, it would have behooved him to listen to us more, but I don't resent or regret anything he did. He was classic. You never had to wonder, "Is he going to be mad?" There was no guessing. If my dad said it, it was law. My father didn't play around, especially when it came to education. I was so used to seeing what he had done with David and Kim, I always knew when I'd get in trouble.

They did a great job disciplining us. We weren't very bad kids, but that's because we knew if we did wrong, we'd pay. Retribution would come. I was petrified of my father. We could go fishing and do all kinds of fun things together, but I knew if I did wrong, I'd get a spanking. People say you're not supposed to be afraid of your parents, but I think it's respect for authority, not fear. People are scared of the police. Why shouldn't you have that same respect for your parents?

We had to own up to our mistakes. I remember one time when I was real young, my brother or sister broke a lamp and when Dad asked who did it, both of them said, "I don't know." So he spanked them both. I remember thinking, "I would have told on whoever broke it." I didn't have any problem telling on them. Sometimes, I'd tell on myself. I'd say, "Dad, I broke the window and I'll pay for it." If we owned up, sometimes he'd surprise us. He'd say, "Okay," and he'd walk upstairs. I'd think he was going to get a belt, but it'd just be done. We learned to come right out and tell our parents when we did something wrong, before the teacher called or they learned the news on their own. We stopped lying, because we knew they hated that. Whether or not we got a spanking, we didn't want to disappoint our parents.

DAVID There were many times I thought they were ogres and that their strictness was ridiculous. As a kid, you look at other kids and you see they're not put on restriction for a bad grade, and they can say all kinds of stuff to their parents and not get spankings, and you think, "Dad, you've been in the military too long. You need to get out. Real people aren't like this."

Now, in retrospect, I wouldn't trade that discipline for anything. Because that was how I developed the discipline I have today. They did a great job of balancing discipline and love.

It's like Chuck says: He always knew that the reason he got spanked was because he did something wrong. He knew what he was doing wrong, and he knew the consequences. That's probably one of the best things my parents did, too. Early on, they were strict and had a lot of guidelines for us, but as we matured, they didn't try to handcuff us. They left a lot of choices up to me, let me use my wisdom, and when I messed up, I knew I had to pay the consequences. We grew up balancing whether to do it right or do it wrong. This worked for us.

94

Chapter Twenty-Two

The Definition and Importance of Discipline

Do not be afraid to discipline your children; to avoid discipline is to invite disaster.

The word *discipline* has developed a negative connotation for a lot of people over the past few decades. They think it's a synonym for physical punishment, and that physical punishment is a synonym for child abuse. This simply isn't true. Physical punishment can be appropriate at times, but it is only one method of discipline.

Discipline is any training and teaching that molds, guides, corrects, and perfects your children. It is essential if you are to raise quality children, and it must be used early and often.

Maybe this is so obvious, it should go without saying, but we mention it because so many parents have been scared off by today's psychologists and politicians. Don't let them bamboozle you. Discipline is a parenting basic that has worked for two thousand years. It goes back to the biblical admonition that if you spare the rod, you will spoil the child. "Rod" can be taken not just in the literal sense, but as a figure of speech for discipline of any kind.

Solomon and the circle of wise men speak to this many times in the book of Proverbs:

Proverbs 13:24: "He who spares the rod hates his son, but he who loves him is careful to discipline him."

Proverbs 19:18: "Discipline your son, for in that there is hope; do not be a willing party to his death."

Proverbs 23:13–14: "Do not withhold discipline from a child; if you punish him with the rod, he will not die. Punish him with the rod and save his soul from death."

Proverbs 29:15: "The rod of correction imparts wisdom, but a child left to himself disgraces his mother."

Proverbs 29:17: "Discipline your son, and he will give you peace."

FREDA All children need love *and* discipline. You don't spare the rod, because you *can* spoil the child. I know that for a fact. Society is confused now and children are going undisciplined, and that's partly why the crime rate is so high. That's why so many children are out of control today. They're going undisciplined at an early age, and when parents try to get them into check later, they can't do it, because that time is past. When they should have started appropriate discipline, they didn't.

Discipline is important. The Holy Scriptures support it. The Bible says if we don't discipline our children, we're treating them as if they were illegitimate, as if we don't love them (Hebrews 12:8). This is why it should be done at an early age.

These are a few of my favorite Scriptures instructing parents how to train their children:

Ephesians 6:4: Fathers, do not exasperate your children; instead, bring them up in the training and instruction of the Lord.

Proverbs 22:6: Train a child in the way he should go, and when he is old he will not turn from it.

Proverbs 22:15: Folly is bound up in the heart of a child, but the rod of discipline will drive it far from him.

Second Timothy 3:15: From infancy you have known the holy Scriptures, which are able to make you wise for salvation through faith in Christ Jesus.

Hebrews 12:7: Endure hardship as discipline; God is treating you as sons. For what son is not disciplined by his father?

Chapter Twenty-Three
Revoking Privileges

───────

Taking away privileges is one effective form of discipline.

Chuck was a smart aleck. He liked to chat, he liked to fool around, and he liked to act up on the long ride to middle school. Finally, the bus driver could take it no longer and told him to knock it off. But Chuck didn't want to be shown up in front of his friends; he wanted to be cool and popular. He mouthed off. This happened more than once, and the driver reported him to the principal's office. The principal told him he was going to call his parents, and suddenly, Chuck was petrified. "Don't tell my mom! Don't tell my dad!" he pleaded. "Give me detention, but don't tell them!"

Too late. His parents were called to the principal's office.

You would not have wanted to be Chuck Robinson that day.

Not when Ambrose Robinson had to miss work for this nonsense.

Not when Freda Robinson had already been to the office once because this same son was cutting up in class.

It was time to play double jeopardy, only this was no game. His parents had already taken away his allowance for misbehaving in class. Now they were going to take away his allowance *and* his privileges. The school was threatening to kick him off the bus for good if he acted up again, and his father told him if the school did, tough luck. Both parents drove to work early in the morning, and they weren't about to take him—or let him hitch a ride with friends, either.

"You will find yourself walking to school thirteen miles each way," Ambrose told his youngest son.

Quickly, Chuck straightened up.

No spankings or beatings were needed. Chuck got the message, because his parents followed through by cutting his allowance and grounding him. He knew they'd follow through on their walk-to-school threat, too.

CHUCK I didn't fear any punishment more than my parents'. My school was thirty minutes away by bus, so it was probably a four-hour walk. He would have made me do it, too. My father was true to his word. He didn't say things in jest.

I remember I missed the bus once after that, and if you missed the bus, you were out of luck. School was so far away, you couldn't get there unless someone took you. So I called my dad in Crystal City and said, "Dad, I missed the bus."

The only thing he said was, "I don't care if you have to walk, you better get to school." And he hung up.

I took a cab. It cost me twenty bucks.

AMBROSE I told Chuck he couldn't ride with his friends in their cars, because when kids start riding with each other, some bad activities can get started. Three or four kids get together and one wants to smoke and they start passing cigarettes around, whereas on the bus, that's controlled. Or if he decides he wants to skip class or leave early, the opportunity is there because he can get out and go and we'll never know about it.

We had two cars and both were for work. Without the car, I couldn't get to work. And I couldn't afford to have one of the children wrecking the car. It was easy to say no. It probably drove them up the wall. Kids want to drive fast, and more than a few people had gone into the ditches around there.

FREDA I never had to go to school for Kim and David unless it was a PTA meeting or an awards ceremony. Ambrose had been a mischievous child, and Chuck started out with his daddy's temper, but I worked with him. He was one of those trying children. You couldn't tell him what was going to happen, you had to show him. He didn't give me any trouble in elementary school, but I had trouble with him in middle school. They knew me down at his middle school.

You had to be careful how you disciplined Chuck. When we'd take away his allowance, he'd say he wasn't born with money, so he could live without it. If we threatened Chuck with physical punishment, he'd tell us, "That's child abuse. You'll be locked up for that." In grade school, we took away his money and privileges. When he got to high school, we took away driving. We just denied his privileges.

AMBROSE It was hard to get Chuck to study. We had to make him bring his books home. He'd come home and I'd ask, "Where are your books?" and he'd say, "In school" and I'd say, "Don't you have homework?" and he'd say, "Yeah," and I'd say, "You better bring those books home next time." This happened more than once. Chuck was rebellious and will readily admit that to you. He told me the other day he couldn't understand how we put up with him back then. The words *born again* really do apply to him now.

They all did mischievous things, but none of them got into big trouble. We tried to teach what was proper and improper to do. Maybe some of it stuck. The little trouble they got into at school was for talking out of turn in class, things like that. But as far as fighting or gang trouble, that problem wasn't there.

KIMBERLY The biggest thing I ever got in trouble for was changing a report card grade. I changed a D to a B or a C. It was obvious I changed it. I was in elementary school, maybe fourth or fifth grade, and I got a good spanking. Now when I look back, I know it was dumb, but my parents were always pushing good grades, and that was my answer.

To be honest, I was the one who didn't get in trouble. When things happened around the house, my parents would say, "Okay, which one of you boys did it? We know Kim didn't do it." They were always in sports and outside activities, so a spanking didn't hurt them nearly as much as being put on restriction.

Chapter Twenty-Four

When Is Physical Punishment Appropriate?

When reason and restriction won't work, sometimes a spanking solves a discipline problem.

The concept of the "timeout chair" wasn't popular when Ambrose and Freda Robinson were raising their children, but they did use the child's bedroom as a "timeout room." The children could be restricted to their rooms for a period of time determined by their act of misbehavior. Or they could be restricted to staying inside the house, or within the property lines. Or they could have part or all of their allowance withheld. Or they could be denied privileges, like going to a movie or game or riding their bikes.

Or they could be spanked with a hand, belt, or switch.

Sometimes parents need to use physical punishment. Much of the new psychology disagrees. Tough love is not really in vogue or politically correct. But the Robinsons believe otherwise. They are convinced that real love is tough love.

AMBROSE You want to get me thrown in jail? In my day, a lot of the things I did to my children were called discipline. These days, some of those punishments would be called child

100

abuse and could probably get me thrown in jail. I didn't try to kill anybody, but I let my kids know, "Look, I mean what I say."

Some of these children today, telling their mothers where to go, I'd have to give them a backhand, because you can't put up with that. There is no room for children to talk back to their parents. I don't talk back to my father even now. Hence the discipline disappears. If you let children do it between the ages of two and five, which is when they learn a lot, by the time they're twelve or thirteen, they'll be animals. And you can see the results just looking around our country now.

I can't totally agree with some of these psychologists who say you'll harm a child's self-esteem or lead him toward a more violent adulthood if you physically punish him. Despite all of this new psychology, I still believe there are times when some sort of physical punishment is necessary to get that child's attention.

FREDA The words "physical punishment" can mean different things to different people. Some will think, "Oh, they just want to punish somebody." I don't want anyone to get the impression I beat up my children. I disciplined them because I loved them. I always told them I did it because I didn't want the policeman to do it.

AMBROSE There are various levels of physical punishment. Acceptable punishment could be a rap on the knuckles, a light spanking, or spanking with a belt or switch. I don't believe in beating kids. Yes, a parent might fly off the handle once in a while, but the most effective enforcement is to be gentle yet firm.

Sometimes you cannot *talk* children out of doing something wrong. You can sit and talk until you're blue in the face, and they'll still do wrong. When talking fails, when they continually repeat an offense that you have preached about, physical punishment can work. Spanking with your hand is okay. If it was serious, I would use a belt or a switch.

What type of behavior deserves a spanking? I wouldn't spank for breaking something. Material things are not worth it.

Well, if you broke it after I told you to be careful, that might deserve a spanking. If you repeated an offense I had warned you about already, maybe the spanking would help you remember the next time. I spanked when my kids did something I told them not to do, and I had explained it more than once. I used spankings as an attention-getter: I need you to listen to me next time. Occasionally I'd spank for mischievous acts—like throwing water on each other, splattering paint on the walls, or knocking over paint cans. All children want to be a little mischievous.

DAVID If I had to name one thing my parents did right, I'd say discipline. A lot of parents don't believe in spankings, and I didn't like them as a kid, but I look back now and I really appreciate the way my parents were able to discipline me and still let me know they loved me. That's a tough balance, and I don't know that a lot of parents succeed at it very well. But my parents did a great job with it.

I look at some of our laws nowadays, and if parents spank a kid at all, they can get in a lot of trouble. But I just don't think you can raise your kids without discipline and respect. A spanking is a whole lot better than putting a kid on punishment for a month. Some think spanking should be a last resort, but I'd much rather get a spanking than lose privileges. Worse than the spanking is the disapproval that comes with it. Kids get a real sense of their parents' disapproval when they get spanked. It's immediate feedback, it's behavior correction, and then it's over, no hard feelings.

Some parents can't control their tempers and spank for the wrong reason. But in our family, it was a discipline thing, not a personal thing. I never felt my dad spanked me because he hated me. I always got the sense he was disciplining me out of love and for a reason.

CHUCK Everything our parents did was biblical. The Bible says not to spare the rod. It says a little chastening now will pay off later. And that's so true. Nobody likes to get a spanking. I hated it. But I remembered it. And like David said, it's immediate feedback. So you knew, "If I do that again, this will happen." It definitely changes your behavior and it teaches you what's right and wrong at an early age. That's the most important thing: doing it at an early age. Once you get a little older, spankings aren't as necessary. Older kids sometimes feel bad just because they know they did wrong, and parents can let it go at that.

My kids will definitely get spanked if they do wrong. I'll do it out of love. That's one thing we knew as kids: We knew our parents loved us, and they wouldn't spank us if we hadn't done wrong. They never spanked us for no reason. Never.

Chapter Twenty-Five

Balancing Love and Discipline

---

*Do not bruise your children's bottoms
or their brains. Be sure to mix love, praise,
and rewards with your discipline.*

FREDA Your children have to understand why you're disciplining them. Discipline right after the offense, so they understand why you did so. Discipline out of love, not anger. How do you make them understand you love them when you are disciplining them? Show them you hate the crime and not the criminal. Address the crime appropriately and objectively. Don't overpunish an infraction.

We gave them a little allowance, incentives but not bribes. And if they didn't do what they were supposed to do, sometimes that allowance would be cut.

AMBROSE We tried to set reasonable expectations and make clear what the point was. When they did something well, we'd stroke them. You can never stroke anybody enough, whether it's at home or in the workplace. If somebody does a good job, you should praise that person. But usually, if you do a good job at the office for four and a half days a week and screw up once, you only hear about the screwup.

I stroked my children when stroking was due. I disciplined them when discipline was due. I didn't yell very much. I didn't have to. I'd look at my children, and they'd know I didn't approve of something. We gave them rewards and incentives: "If you clean up your room, I'll give you so and so." That's giving them the carrot *and* the stick.

FREDA Ambrose gave them a lot of treats, such as taking them to circuses and so many things other children did not get to do. We sacrificed other things to make sure they were exposed to a lot and got to enjoy a lot of privileges, a lot of trips. When we chose the things to do, we wanted things they could learn from. Ambrose was a softie when it came to taking the children to anything educational. We took them bowling, we took them to movies, and we ate out a lot.

A rich man's agenda might be playing tennis or taking the children to eat at a country club. We couldn't afford that. Eating out on a Friday night was a treat. A lot of times we'd go to all-you-can-eat places because they liked to eat.

Chapter Twenty-Six

Leave 'em Laughing

---

*Developing a sense of humor helps
make for a well-rounded person who's fun
to be around.*

Today, all the Robinsons can tell funny stories about growing up, or trade funny barbs at the bowling alley. But when he was small, David was more reserved and analytical than most children his age. Sometimes the tongue-in-cheek subtleties of sarcasm were lost on him.

FREDA It seemed like David was involved in every sport, and I was the one who had to drive him around. I thought there was no end to it. Then he'd volunteer me to drive everyone else everywhere in the station wagon, and it would frustrate me because these other children's parents should have been doing something. I probably shouldn't have felt like that, but I worked every day. I was *tired*!

On top of that, it seemed as if he was always bringing home a note asking, "Gimme, gimme, gimme." One November he said, "The teacher wants us to bring in four cans for the Thanksgiving basket, and she wants us to nominate names of poor families, and then they'll select five names for the Thanksgiving baskets."

I was so tired of those children bringing home donation requests, I said, "Every time I turn around, it's give, give, give. This is the poor house right here. Our name needs to be in the basket."

I was being sarcastic, but he took me seriously. He went to the school and put my name in the basket. And wouldn't you know it: My name came up as one of the five names!

The teacher knew me and called me. She said, "Freda, you're trying to be slick. Why did you have David put your name in for a poor basket?"

I said, "What? I didn't know anything about that!"

He had taken me literally. He thought we needed a basket.

He didn't stop at that. He went up to the church and put our name in with the Sunday school teacher, Barbara Mann. When I got to church, Barbara met me and said, "Freda, we caught you."

I said, "What?"

She said, "David put your name in for a Thanksgiving basket. He tried to pull it off, but it didn't work."

I said, "Barbara, honest to goodness, I am telling the truth, I did not tell him to put my name in for that basket."

She said, "I figured that. I took it right out because it had no business being in there."

David said, "Mama, I was only trying to help. You told me this was the poor house."

Part Three
High School and Teenage Angst

Chapter Twenty-Seven
We Shall Overcome

It's good to recognize racism past and present, but to dwell on it, to rail against it, can be self-defeating.

Ambrose Robinson and his brother Kenneth blossomed from boys to men in Little Rock, Arkansas in the late fifties and early sixties, a loathsome period in America that most people would just as soon we forget. Ambrose and Freda Robinson would just as soon young children never know the callous racism they endured. But they also know it is important for teens and adults, blacks and whites, to understand whence we have come, lest we repeat the mistakes of the past.

To many of us, those turbulent times are just scenes out of movies such as *Mississippi Burning* or TV shows such as *I'll Fly Away*. But the Robinsons lived them. Ambrose could have been one of the so-called Little Rock Nine who first integrated Central High, but then vetoed the idea for fear of the violence that indeed arose when Arkansas Governor Orval Faubus ordered the Arkansas National Guard to bar blacks from Central High. Claiming he feared riots if blacks were admitted, Faubus defied the Supreme Court order to end segregation in public schools and reopened the schools as private, segregated schools. When President Dwight D. Eisenhower could not persuade Faubus to obey the law of the land, he finally sent in federal troops to protect black students as they integrated the schools.

The ugliness forced Ambrose to miss school his entire junior year—he could only take correspondence courses, with no physics or chemistry because he couldn't attend labs—before entering all-black Horace Mann as a senior. Still, he scored so highly on his college entrance exams, he was accused of cheating. Blacks weren't supposed to be that smart. Forced to take the test again, he was locked alone in a room with four proctors hovering over his shoulders—and scored even higher.

Kenneth, six years younger, survived threats, intimidation, and violence to become the first black basketball player at Central. When Central played at neighboring North Little Rock, his father was not allowed to watch. "I don't care who you or your son are, you are not coming in this gym," the doorman told him and blocked the door.

Growing up in Columbia, South Carolina, Freda couldn't drink at the "white" water fountain and faced nasty store clerks who would ignore her and wait on whites who stood in line behind her. She sought jobs that were advertised in the paper, was told there were no openings, and then watched the white women behind her get the jobs.

Ambrose and Freda have seen enough to make even the most saintly bitter, yet when they married, they made a pact that their children would not suffer a second-class education or second-class treatment. Their children would attend the best schools even if it meant they would be isolated from people of their own color. They would shelter their children from some racial realities because they wanted them to grow up with positive attitudes. They would rather their children grow up in a fantasy world than cripple them with militance, anger, and defiance.

They know racism and racial tensions still exist. They know the grim statistics: Forty-eight percent of all black families are headed by women. The unemployment rate for black males is twice that of whites while the college graduation rate is half that of whites. The murder rate for African-American males is fourteen times that of the rest of society. The proportion of black males ages twenty to twenty-nine imprisoned, on probation, or on parole has grown from one in four to one in three in just the past five years. They hope their advice can help the many black families in crisis, can help everyone understand the slights blacks still face in a white world.

But they rarely told their children of the racism they faced, never made it an issue, never made it an excuse, never gave them a chance to get angry.

AMBROSE My brother and I had to fight for everything we got and had to accept limited gain in lieu of the usual opportunities afforded others—opportunities which, a generation later, were there for David Robinson. David's own life has become an extension of his family's. David has seemed to receive what was denied to my brother and me—a curious extension of fate or at least poetic justice.

I was a good high school basketball player, one of the best around. That's one reason I was supposed to go to the University of Arkansas: They saw my potential. I was good enough to play for the team, but not to live with the white players. So I went to Tuskegee Institute instead, but back in those days, if you went to a black college, you didn't get much of a chance to go to the NBA.

Kenneth came along six years later and got that chance. He attended the University of Denver and spent a year with the New Orleans Jazz and another with the Harlem Globetrotters. If I could have converted my time from 1959 to 1966, I might have been in the NBA, too. I was 6'7½" ahead of my time like Julius Erving. I could dunk and do all kinds of things. I could play outside or inside. I could shoot three-pointers or play center. My coach was O.B. Elders, a once famous Globetrotter. His wife is Jocelyn Elders, who went on to become surgeon general. Chuck and David didn't believe all the things I told them I did, but when they went back and talked to the coach, O.B. told them, "He was the man." And they looked at me and said, "Pops, you were all right, huh?" I was, but I just happened to be in the wrong place at the wrong time.

113

FREDA I came through that era. Whites didn't want you around them. I was bussed almost twenty miles every day, past about six white schools, so they could send me to a black school. All we got were the raggedy books the white kids had torn up. This was our *society*, our *government* promoting racism! They had a tizzy when they found out there'd be integration.

Ambrose told me about what happened with the Little Rock Nine, and I read about it, but I never really knew how much those kids went through, how they were tortured, by adults as well as children, until I saw the Ernest Green story in a TV movie. White parents calling black kids all kinds of racist slurs, telling them they did not want them there, their place was with other niggers. White kids pushing a black girl down the stairs, causing them to take classes in a black lady's house. Even the principal was so prejudiced, it was a disgrace. Before I gave my life to the Lord, I probably would have gotten a gun and blown them away if they had mistreated my kids like that. I had to get up and turn off the TV, that's how bad it was. It was just too traumatic. I experienced some things, but nothing like that. It was a disgrace, a national disgrace. They hated people just because of the color of their skin.

Then I could understand why Ambrose was always telling the children, "You *can* do it. There's no such thing as *can't* in our house. You *can* do it. I *know* you can do it."

Times have changed a lot, but then again, not a lot. Racism is still there; it's just not as evident today. It's undercover. I can see why people give up and say, "I'm not going to be anything." I can understand why people become real militant and bitter.

You need Jesus Christ to sustain you through trials like that. That's why I say God can give you a peace that man can't take away from you. If you believe in God, people can spit on you, and you can take it with a smile instead of slapping their head off.

AMBROSE When we decided to buy our first home in the early seventies, we met with several realtors, and the last one really upset me. We found this nice three-bedroom home with a list price of about $26,000 and he told me I couldn't afford it based on our income. I knew we could, and I was furious, because I figured they obviously didn't want people of color in this new neighborhood. We went a few miles away to another new development and met another realtor and found a home we liked even better for $32,500. Our loan was approved, and we moved to the Green Run subdivision in 1973.

FREDA When we moved to Green Run, there were only two black families in that neighborhood. We made three. I don't think there were ten blacks in the whole school. The whites would isolate you. What they failed to realize was we didn't want to be around them either, if they were racists. When you are a victim of racism, you can smell the stench of prejudice. This is why I didn't want my children to be raised with militance or hatred. We taught them the world doesn't owe you anything just because a hundred years ago there were slaves.

You can't feel sorry for yourself. You have to help yourself. You don't worry about the racists out there. You don't let them affect you. That's why it's so important for our children to have self-esteem. I always told my children, "If your self-esteem is high enough, no one can take it away from you. And if you don't have any self-esteem, a dog can make you feel like nothing." You have to know within yourself that you're just as good as anyone else.

Ambrose told our kids, "Listen, you can do anything. You can be president of the United States. You can be an ambassador. You can be anybody you want to be. Don't let anybody tell you because you're black you can't do something. You can do anything if you study and you apply yourself. Nobody can take that out of your hands or your brains."

A reporter asked me recently, "Why did you shelter David?" It wasn't so much that we sheltered him. But there's a thin line there, and when you think about mistreatment, you can very well start to hate. I'd rather them be too sheltered than not sheltered enough. So we didn't talk about it much when they were small. When they were older, they could handle it better. We raised the racism issue, but we didn't focus on it because nothing about racism is positive. We wanted to reinforce the positives and avoid the negatives, because I did not want them to grow up militant. Because I knew what it was to grow up in hate, real hate. I grew up in South Carolina, and trust me, South Carolina could be bitter, real bitter.

It wasn't that Ambrose and I were color-blind, that our children didn't know prejudice existed, it's just that they didn't know how bad it was. Because anything you reinforce just sinks in deeper. We never tried to reinforce racism. Why reinforce a bad dream? So they'd have nightmares? To become angry and militant is crippling. I would much rather have them live in a world of fantasy than to be crippled.

It's not all about prejudice. Part of it is just getting along with other people. It's getting along with the world. Some things you just need to do. If I sit in this house and focus on a bad experience with my husband instead of saying, "He bought me roses the other day," I'm dwelling on the negative. I refuse to do it. It's a sickness. If someone asks, I'll say, "My husband is wonderful," even if I had just disagreed with him.

Chapter Twenty-Eight

Can-Do Attitude

Make sure you instill positive attitude and high self-esteem, because they are essential to success.

You don't want praise to be bogus—you want to be a coach, not just a cheerleader—but you need to compliment your children and instill a positive attitude. In fact, a can-do attitude isn't just for children; it's good for people of all ages and races.

Eleanor Roosevelt said it: "No one can make you feel inferior without your consent."

Marian Wright Edelman said it: "Be a can-do, will-try person. America is being paralyzed by can't-doers with puny vision and punier wills. . . . You are in charge of your own attitude. Whatever others do or whatever circumstances you face, the only person you can control is yourself."

Even "The One Minute Manager" advises bosses to "catch" their employees doing something right; this is the key to developing people.

AMBROSE I've always tried to use positive language. There are no such words and never were such words as *I can't* in my household. I never believed in complaining and gossiping. It leads to unhealthy attitudes and situations.

I saw the children do a lot of things right, and I'd compliment them. Often it was just saying a few words but putting emphasis on them: "Good job! Great job! Super job!" Sometimes it would be taking them to buy a burger. I wasn't a fast-food freak, but say they had done a great job on their chores or schoolwork, for a special treat we'd go to McDonald's or Burger King. I didn't believe in always giving them rewards for good grades, but I'd stroke them when they came home with great grades. I'd point out the bad things first, then always try to end on a positive note.

If I had to do it again, I would give my kids even more positive strokes. Kids need to know when they're doing things right. And you just can't make it phony; that's the downside of stroking.

FREDA You've got to make children believe they can do the job, that they can compete with anybody. You've got to say, "Well done, great, great job. This house is cleaner than any I've seen." They like it. They eat it up. You take your wife. You might say, "You look really nice today," and she might not say anything, but believe me, inside she's feeling good. Sometimes you just need that little compliment. At least show you noticed. It's like David told Ed Bradley on *60 Minutes*: "If you can make children believe they can do anything, then they can."

I always told them when they were small, "You guys will be great. You will get your education. We want you to go further than Mom and Dad. If you keep doing what you're doing now, you're one-eighth of the way there."

They'd look up at me and say, "Mom, you think so?"

And I'd say, "You did a great job, a great job."

And they'd say, "Oh, you're the best mom. We've got the best mom of all."

You've got to help your children believe in themselves. If you keep complimenting them and building them up, then when you need to criticize, if you do it constructively, you've won them. All they want to know is, "My dad and mom love me." What child doesn't want to be loved?

Now, David has such a positive attitude, if the Spurs lose and he's played his heart out, do you think he points a finger?

No way! It's not just for good PR or team unity, either. He'll come over to our house, and I'll be burned up about the loss, and he won't say anything bad about anyone. I've heard people interviewing him try every kind of way to get him to say something negative and this is what he'll say: "That's interesting." Last year they were trying to get him to talk about Dennis Rodman (harming the Spurs' playoff chances) and he said, "I love him." And he wasn't lying. One reporter said, "How can you love somebody who causes all these problems?" He said, "I love him like a brother. I have to respect him for himself. I don't particularly like all the things he does, but I have no control over that." He is just so *sweet*, you've got to love him. He just doesn't doubt folks.

Chapter Twenty-Nine

When You Can't Do

*Help your children understand the dif-
ference between quitting something and
being a quitter.*

David Robinson was frustrated. He was in ninth grade, his
last year of middle school, and he was showing up for basketball practice every day, but rarely playing. He knew his father
didn't like quitters, but he thought he should quit the team.

Finally, he went to Ambrose and said, "Dad, I'm not getting
any playing time. The only time they put me in is when we're
twenty points up and there's two minutes left and it doesn't
make sense for me to play."

Ambrose had gone to the games. He knew the score. He
thought his son was a little better than the coach did, but he
didn't believe in interfering. Now, if David were playing a lot and
wanted to quit because he wasn't doing well, that would have
been different. But he wasn't playing and wasn't having fun, and
if he'd rather study than shoot hoops, why, Dad wasn't about to
argue with those priorities. The conversation lasted all of one
or two minutes.

"Fine," Ambrose said. "You don't have to play."

David sought out his mom to tell her.

"David," she asked, "are you quitting because you're
embarrassed not to be playing?"

"No," he said, "I feel my talent is being wasted. I'm not being utilized. I don't want to be a bench warmer. It's a waste of my time."

If he wanted to quit because the coach upset or intimidated him, Freda would have suggested he explain his feelings to the coach first. And if he wanted to quit something really important, like school, that would have been different. But his answer satisfied her.

Freda and Ambrose did not accept quitters in their family. Persistence, perseverance, tenacity, never say die—call it whatever you want, but it's a key ingredient for the success of any person, young or old. Still, there's a difference between quitting something and being a quitter in life. Sometimes you need to know when to quit. You keep climbing to the top of Kilimanjaro even if you're a little sore, but not if your limbs are frozen and you risk gangrene and amputation. You keep working hard at a school subject or a sport and maybe you'll get the hang of it, but if the course is an elective or the sport isn't essential and you'll never get anything but frustration out of it, you can quit.

FREDA It took a little guts to quit. Some people would have not said anything, would have been intimidated. Not David. I understood his reasoning, and I didn't think it was fair to make him sit on the bench when he felt like his talent was being wasted.

David was a little disillusioned with sports after that. He said, "I can always make the team in any sport, but I don't want to just make the team. I want to play." Most people consider it an achievement just to make the team, but that wasn't enough for him.

DAVID To quit playing was one of the hardest things I ever did as a kid. It stuck with me, too. That team went on to win the city championship. It was a good team. I just remember that experience and how hard it was for me to quit during the season. That was the first thing I ever quit. I did not make the decision lightly.

Now, when I talk with kids, I always talk about persistence and perseverance. I tell them, "Being a quitter in life is a whole lot different than having setbacks and having to quit sometimes. Sometimes you have to stop. But when you have an attitude of perseverance, you may run into a wall, but with creativity and persistence, you can get through it." Obviously, I've run into walls, but I've been able to get through a lot of them.

AMBROSE I did not want my children to be quitters. I believe there's no such thing as "I can't." If you tackle a project, you can finish a project. And you can be the best at whatever you choose to do. David preaches that today. He says even if you're collecting garbage, be the best garbage man you can be.

FREDA To be a quitter is to be a loser. I don't think of David as ever being a loser. Sometimes you need to quit things. If you can recognize the line that says, "Quit now while you're ahead," you'll be okay. I always listened to my children's reasoning. They had a right to make their own choices. If they had a good enough reason, okay. But if it was not the right reason, then I questioned it. I never worried a lot about sports; I was harder on the regular curriculum. That was first and foremost.

Chapter Thirty
Finding Sports Success

High school athletes make the pros about as often as regular lottery players win million-dollar jackpots. Enjoy the sport, but don't bet all your money on such a risky gamble.

David didn't play basketball again until he was a senior—and then only because of homesickness, or maybe fate.

After Ambrose retired from the Navy, he took a job consulting on government contracts in Crystal City, Virginia, just outside Washington, D.C. and about 185 miles from home in Virginia Beach. He lived in an apartment during the week and commuted home on weekends for about a year before buying a house in Woodbridge, Virginia, about twenty-five miles south of D.C. On Halloween in 1982, the family moved.

Everyone except David, that is. He stayed behind in Virginia Beach and lived with a family friend.

Ambrose just assumed that David wanted to stay behind with his peers and not disrupt his senior year in one of the nation's best school districts, and David was too obedient to speak up. But Freda figured David would excel wherever he went to school and that he needed his family more than he did his friends. She cried the night they left David behind, and she

123

continued to question the wisdom of their decision when their son woke up early every morning before school to call his mom.

Finally, his godmother said, "Freda, David is homesick. He's lonesome. Ask him if he wants to come live with you."

The next morning when David called, Freda asked him if he wanted to move to Woodbridge. She had barely gotten the question out of her mouth when he said, "Yes, ma'am."

Excited, Freda called her husband with the news.

"Why are you calling me? Just go get him," Ambrose replied.

She called David back. "I'll be down there in three hours. Tell the guidance counselor I said to get all your papers together because you're moving."

"Oh, yes, ma'am," David said, and Freda could hear the happiness in his voice. She raced to Virginia Beach and found him with his bags packed and his paperwork complete.

"Mama," he said in the car, "I'm so glad you came. I missed you."

David never volunteered his feelings before he was asked them; he was too eager to please, too compliant to his parents' wishes. The mistake, Ambrose says now, was *assuming* what David wanted instead of *asking*.

The next day, Ambrose took David to Garfield High School a few blocks away, only to learn the area had been rezoned and David would have to go to Osbourne Park High. This appeared to be bad news; Osbourne Park was thirteen miles away. But again, fate was on the Robinsons' side. As it turned out, Garfield was a bigger school, with a rougher crowd of teens. And at Osbourne Park, David soon discovered that his guidance counselor was also the varsity basketball coach. Art Payne took one look at this gangling 6'7" senior and asked him to try out for the team. David promised he would, and for the rest of the day, student after student approached him, each one saying the same words: "You've got to play basketball. You've got to play basketball." Everyone was so enthusiastic, he couldn't say no.

He watched the team work out and made a few shots in his stocking feet that day, then got his physical and started practicing the next day. When the starting center sprained his ankle, David was thrust into the starting job despite his lack of experience. He found basketball to be more work than it was fun. Payne placed him near the basket to take advantage of his height, but he was knocked around by stronger, more aggressive players, and the coach could tell the kid's heart was not really into it. Fortunately, Payne was understanding and sensitive and didn't push too hard. He brought in a former college center to help David learn the basics of post play, and David averaged about fourteen points a game and was voted to the All-Metro second team, All-Area and All-District teams. But he didn't think he had a future in the game, and he was not alone in his opinion.

"He was a skinny 6'7" kid who did okay because he was tall," recalled Mike Dufrene, who played against him in preps and college. "To compare him then to where he is now, that's something that should be on *Amazing Stories* or *That's Incredible*."

David played baseball that year, too, and his father considered that his better sport. He was a first baseman and an imposingly tall, fast left-handed pitcher. But he wasn't necessarily the most accomplished high school athlete in the family. Kim had played two years of varsity tennis, and Chuck would not only play football, but go to the state championship in two track events, make the all-city basketball team as a junior, and average more than twenty points a game as a senior, earning multiple scholarship offers.

Only a dreamer could have predicted David would become an All-American in three years, College Player of the Year in four years, NBA Rookie of the Year in six years.

AMBROSE David was okay as a basketball player. I was one of the few if not the only one who saw a little athletic potential in him. I figured, "This guy could be good if he put his mind to it." He had some attention-span problems, but then he'd go on five minute spurts where you'd see he had the makings of a player.

125

I liked sports and enjoyed playing with the children and watching them play, but I never pushed sports on them. I never tried to build them into athletes. I've heard about how the old Oakland Raider, Marv Marinovich, tried to build his son Todd into an athlete by bringing in all kinds of expert coaches, by never letting him eat junk food or drink a soda, but I never did anything like that. People ask me: "What did you feed David as a kid?" I say, "Whatever was on the table. If you didn't eat it, you went to bed hungry." We had no rules about junk food. Being a jack of all trades, I showed my kids how to throw a football, how to play baseball and softball and basketball. I didn't need to hire anybody to do that.

We didn't even shoot much together when David was in high school. The only times we got serious was when David was in college and Chuck was in middle school. David would come home from Navy, and we'd go to the local high school or a place outside our church, and we'd shoot around and play a few pickup games. I'd go one on one with both David and Chuck. After getting hit two or three times in the head and getting my teeth knocked out, I decided not to bother with that anymore.

Athletics, as far as I was concerned, was not the way to go. Education was. That was instilled into me, and that's what I instilled into my kids.

Sports was just an outlet, something to do for rest and relaxation. We never looked at it as a possible livelihood. I think that is a mistake some parents make these days. They're playing baseball and football in the backyard, hoping their children will become pro sports heroes when they grow up. That's not the way to do it, in my opinion. If it happens, all's well and good. But I don't think you can groom a pro athlete. You talk to numerous pro athletes, and they'll tell you they had no idea when they were youngsters that they'd be playing pro sports. They might have emulated certain heroes, but I don't think parents should push it because such a small percentage who try to go pro make it.

Usually, you don't really know if a kid has a chance at a pro career until sometime during college. I didn't really think David had a chance until the end of his sophomore or middle of his junior year, when he was seven feet tall and averaging more than twenty points a game. Maybe with some kids you can tell in high school, but that's one in a hundred thousand. If he's 6'6" in sixth grade, maybe he's got a chance. If he's Shawn Bradley, growing to be 7'7", he's got potential to be in the league ten or twelve years. Even when we thought David had a shot at the pros, the only thing we did differently was consider whether he should leave Navy and his five-year commitment and transfer to a basketball factory.

Chapter Thirty-One
Building the TV and the Man

*Help your children develop multiple
talents and interests that will prepare them
to become well-rounded adults.*

Education was always the top priority in the Robinson household. But by the time the children reached high school, they knew education wasn't restricted to the classroom. All learned lessons in the sports they played. All learned lessons about work ethic. David and Chuck delivered papers and mowed lawns. Kimberly baby-sat and worked in fast-food restaurants. David played the piano, and Chuck sang in a rap group. David had his father's love of music, math, and engineering, and took advanced math and computer courses.

And, just before he turned sixteen, he put together a wide-screen TV from a kit. It can still be found in the Woodbridge home.

FREDA David's daddy bought the Heathkit for both of them to build after he got back from his two or three weeks of exercises at sea. The kit was sitting in the den in a big box and when I got home from the dispensary one day, Kim met me at the car and said, "Mom! I tried to stop him! David is in a world of trouble!"

I said, "What happened?"

DAVID ROBINSON

50 ROBINSON

CENTER OF ATTENTION

Long before he became the NBA's Most Valuable Player, David Robinson was the center of attention of his parents, Ambrose and Freda Robinson *(previous page)*.

The Robinsons are equally proud of the achievements of their son, Chuck, and daughter, Kimberly.

David jams on his alto sax, one of his favorite pastimes *(inset)*.

Parents Ambrose and Freda Robinson wish David well on his wedding day.

Ambrose and Freda outside the San Antonio home that David gave them *(inset)*.

© *60 Minutes.*

Chuck Robinson, David's best man and brother, offers congratulations on his wedding day *(inset)*.

Chuck and David clown around at home in Woodbridge, Virginia, where David played high school basketball for the first time as a senior and Chuck was a sixth grader.

© Brenda For Photography

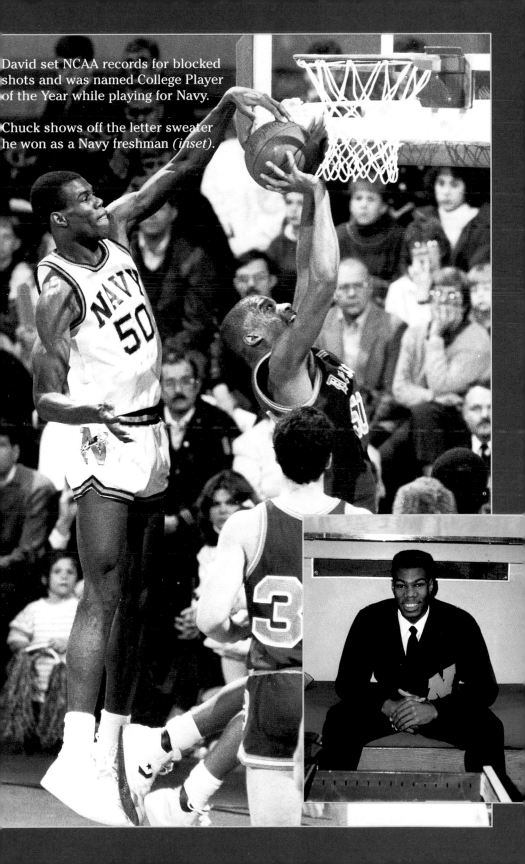

David set NCAA records for blocked shots and was named College Player of the Year while playing for Navy.

Chuck shows off the letter sweater he won as a Navy freshman *(inset)*.

David, Valerie, and their two sons, David Jr. and Corey.

© Brenda For Photography

© Langm

David stands next to his mom and some of the fifth graders he adopted for the I Have a Dream scholarship program.

David shares God's rich blessings with various Christian and youth organizations.

David dances with his mom on his wedding day.

The Robinson parenting skills are being passed down to a new generation *(inset)*.

© Brenda For Photography

She said, "He went into that box and he's messing with Daddy's television."

I said, "He and his daddy will build it when his daddy gets back."

She said, "No, Mom, you don't understand. He's got a whole board done."

It wasn't a $25 kit. It cost a lot of money, something like $400, $500, $600, $700.

I said, "David, do you know how much that kit cost?"

He said, "But Mom, I know what I'm doing."

He just kept working on it while we were talking.

I said, "Your daddy is gonna kill you."

He said, "I'll take the responsibility."

I said, "You better not solder on that board unless you're absolutely sure, because it will be ruined if you're wrong."

He said, "Mom, you worry too much."

Eventually, he soldered everything together and said, "I'm finished. I'm just waiting for Daddy to come back, and then we can light it off."

I went to pick his daddy up at the ship, and I knew he'd be upset. I was hyper. I said, "Honey, don't get mad, but David put your kit together."

He said, "Oh, I wouldn't worry about it. He knows what he's doing."

I said, "But do you know how much this thing costs?"

We got back to the house and Ambrose checked everything and said, "It looks okay."

But David said they were missing a piece, and he was right. Ambrose checked to see if David had put something in the wrong place, and he hadn't. Ambrose went to the Heathkit store to get the piece and the people said, "*He* put it together?" They admitted the piece was missing, Ambrose went back home, put the piece in, and it worked.

AMBROSE I wasn't that upset. I was glad to see it was done and be able to sit down and watch it. We ended up watching what I thought was the best-looking picture on a six-foot screen I had seen to date.

After we finished, we needed a few other spare parts, so we went to the Heathkit store. David saw a demonstration unit in operation and began telling the technician what the problem was. The technician made the changes David suggested—and then it worked nicely.

Chapter Thirty-Two

Leader of the Pack

*Give your child the confidence to talk
with people and lead them.*

Ambrose and Freda Robinson were confident, outgoing people, and it seemed to naturally follow that their children had little trouble striking up conversations and friendships. Because they were given chores and compliments at an early age, because they accomplished things both inside and outside the classroom, they grew up confident in their ability to do a lot of things well. The more confidence they had, the more easily they made friends, and the more those friends showed confidence in them. The neighborhood kids viewed David as a leader long before he became a star athlete.

AMBROSE I can remember some Saturday mornings, children from around the neighborhood would come over to our house and ask David, "What do we do today?" I'm not talking one or two; I'm talking ten or twelve children. And David would tell them, and they'd do whatever he suggested. It was wild. If you met some of those friends now, they'd tell you the same thing. They looked up to him because he always seemed to know what to do.

Self-confidence and leadership go hand in hand. If you don't have self-confidence, you can't be a leader. Self-confidence

131

is a learned thing, part of all the other things we've been talking about, like responsibility, positive attitude, and pats on the back.

Self-confidence helps you live your life. For example, if you're afraid of the sand, I guarantee you, when your golf ball lands in the sand, you'll hit a bad shot. But if you have confidence you'll get out, you'll do okay. You'll hear it when I'm playing golf: "Maintain a positive attitude." Or "There's no sense getting upset." Or "It's just a game."

FREDA When you're talking about leadership, you're talking about take-charge children. That stems from giving them responsibility. Our kids grew up with a take-charge attitude, a feeling of being responsible. They had no choice. They had two parents who worked, so everyone had chores, and we'd check and compliment them if they did good jobs. That's some of the groundwork. You can't make a leader out of someone who isn't a good follower. That comes from good discipline. Undisciplined people don't make good leaders.

Every single one of our kids has confidence. Chuck is very assertive; he has to be in the call-the-shots chair. When Kim interviewed for her teaching job, she sold herself. She told them, "I'm the person for the job. I'll do the best job for you." I said, "You told those people you'd do the best job when you didn't even know who the other candidates were?" She said, "Mom, I need that job and I'm the person for the job. I'll learn from the job, and I can produce for them because of my background. If they don't hire me, I'm still the best person for the job." And she got the job.

Chapter Thirty-Three

Freedom from Religion? No!

Keep faith in the family, even if teens are beginning to question its value. Teens might not be mature enough to make their own choices about going to church, and what they do and do not believe.

FREDA When they were small, it was unstated, it was understood—they would go to Bible studies and church on worship days. So it became a way of life. When they were older, they were more of their own mind. They asked in no uncertain terms, "Do we have to go?" And I'd say, "Yes, I think you do. You owe it to the Lord. He's been good to you this week." I'd put it that way rather than say, "You better get in that car." I knew they could rebel if I forced them to do enough things. They'd tell me point-blank sometimes, "We don't want to go, but if you want us to go, we will."

They were expected to go to church every Sunday as long as they lived in my house. I thought about that a lot, because a lady once told me she thought it was wrong to make teenagers go to church. She said they have a right not to go if they don't want to go. I said, "Whatever happened to guidance? You could leave them home and something could happen to them there when they weren't doing what would have been a better thing for them to do. Which is worse? Requiring them to go to church, or leaving them alone where they can do anything they want? When I'm at church and they're alone, that's idle time. It's a short time to give to the Lord."

133

I didn't make them go if they were sick. A lot of times they'd get slick on me and say they had a headache or stomachache or something. I'd say, "Okay, but sick people don't have any activities. If we go skating or bowling, or if we go to get ice cream, you're not going." And usually they'd say, "Well, maybe I'd better try to go." I could remember playing sick myself on my mother. I'd tell them, "I've done this myself. I know the symptoms." Or I'd say, "Maybe I better take you to the dispensary to see the doctor." They'd say, "Mom, it's just a headache. I can take an aspirin." If they really felt too tired to go, I might let them stay home. But I'd say, "When I come home, you better be in the house and not outside playing."

Ambrose didn't have an answer when they asked, "Why do we have to go if Dad doesn't?" At first, when they said it, it hit home. I couldn't say anything. And so I prayed about it. A good while later they said it again. I said, "Well, I want you to give God praise for what he has done for you, and you might learn something you don't already know. We all need the Lord, and I ask very little of you, but this is one thing I'm asking you to do. I'm not sending you; I'm taking you with me. One or two hours is not that long." They'd frown, but they'd go.

I don't think I'd do it differently today. I know many people will disagree, but these were my convictions. A lot of times you're asking for trouble when you cave in on your convictions. I might let them stay home once or twice if they really didn't want to go. I'd say, "Since you're so insistent on staying home, I'm going to leave you here. But I want you to pray." I'd stress how much they should be doing this, what this would mean to them years later, even though it might not look like anything now.

Making them go to church all those years could have been the reason they didn't go that often in college. But if they hadn't gone in high school, they would have been even more prone to staying home later. Once you miss one Sunday, you don't care if you miss the next Sunday or not. Staying home gets to be a habit, and it's easier not to go at all if you're not going regularly. Now, they all go regularly, and they have all been saved, and I attribute that to the seeds planted when they were young.

Chapter Thirty-Four

Freedom from Curfews? Maybe!

Curfews can backfire. Don't impose strict curfews unless teens abuse the privilege of staying out.

AMBROSE My dad restricted me. You know how there'll be a 10 o'clock curfew on some girls? I had one, too, and I hated it. I swore I'd never put those kinds of restrictions on my children. It was demeaning to me, saying I couldn't stay out until midnight, that I had to leave a fun party at 10 P.M. when it probably didn't even start until 8 or 9 and would last until 1 A.M. I was mischievous to begin with, but one reason I got into trouble was I rebelled against my curfews. I wanted to show people I could do something wrong even with a curfew. I probably did some things I wouldn't have normally done just in retaliation for what my parents were making me miss—like the end of a party. And when I got away to college and didn't have a curfew anymore, I really rebelled. I was wild as a buck rabbit because I hadn't been exposed to a lot of things, and I wanted to do them all at once.

My children knew they should be back around a certain time. On school nights, they'd have to be home by 10:30 P.M., because they'd have to be up by 5:30 A.M. to get to class. But I tried not to make it mandatory, tried not to say, "You will be back at X time, and you will be punished if you're not." It wasn't strictly enforced. I didn't sit around waiting up for them. But I could hear car doors close and the front door opening and closing, and occasionally, I'd look out the window to see who was coming in or whose car they were getting out of. I didn't check up on them that much, but if they told me they were going to the ballfield and I happened to drive by and they weren't there, they'd be in trouble. It never happened.

FREDA Ambrose didn't set real strict curfews, because he thought his daddy went overboard and it only made children more defiant. My parents were the same way. My father was *soooo* strict, the girls in my high school made fun of us. My sister and I would walk into a club and our classmates would point at us and announce, "Those are the Hayes girls. They have to be home by 11." They were telling the truth. They knew we had to hurry out by 10:30.

When we raised our children, the troubles were out there in the world, but we didn't live in the inner city. We were either in base housing, which is well patrolled and well lighted, or in homes that were further out from the city. We took them away from the turmoils of the city. But I wouldn't do a lot different today. I still don't believe in setting a real strict curfew. I liked to give my children the opportunity to come home at a reasonable hour as long as they didn't abuse it. Kids need to have some choice, unless they've exhibited they're not capable of handling it.

If they abuse the privilege, that's a different story. I don't cotton to staying out until 2 or 3 A.M. That's an abuse for a little sixteen-year-old. Or going out with somebody twenty-one years old? Oh, no, no, no. The amount of responsibility and leeway you give them depends on their maturity level. Can you show me you're responsible enough?

CHUCK My senior year, they never gave me a specific curfew. Once I got to high school, I got straight A's. It could be a Tuesday night and I'd say, "Dad, I'd like to go to this party," and he'd say, "Is your homework done?" and I'd say, "Yes," and he'd say, "Okay." He wouldn't tell me what time to come home. He'd just say, "Don't act like a monkey. Act like a human. Be home before I wake up." That was enough. I still wouldn't come home at 4 in the morning. I'd be home by 1 or earlier, but it's that kind of freedom that develops an independent spirit where you're finally able to live on your own.

Chapter Thirty-Five

Sex and Drugs

Explain the dangers, and make sure
your children know they can talk to you
and depend upon you if they slip.

It is no revelation that sex and drugs are major problems facing today's youth. What's a parent to do? You can't chaperone them twenty-four hours a day. You can't pick their friends.

But you can guide them. Long before they reach the vulnerable age of adolescence, you can instill morals and educate them about risks. You can stress that they don't have to give in to peer pressure, that they should not forfeit their future to a foolish friend who cares less about them than you do. You can get to know their friends and their friends' families a little, and while forbidding friendships can often backfire, you can subtly steer them toward safer friends.

AMBROSE I never really screened our childrens' friends. I never saw anyone I didn't like or said a certain child couldn't come back to the house again. We lived in decent neighborhoods, and there weren't as many bad things going on in those days. You weren't afraid the friends were casing your house. I would be more careful today, but it's hard to tell who's a good kid and who's bad. How can you tell if a person is a future convict? The more you tell a teen not to do something or hang out with somebody, the more he wants to.

But you want your children to pick the right friends. It's good to become familiar with their friends and their friends' families, which is something parents don't tend to do as much these days. But it can pay off. I'd tell Chuck something I thought he should do, but he might disagree, so he'd ignore me. Then I'd tell one of Chuck's friends or friend's parent, and that person would suggest it to Chuck and Chuck would say, "Oh, that's a good idea." Sometimes teens will believe somebody else before they believe you. I used that trick a few times.

FREDA We talked to our kids about sex. We told them the consequences. When you have teenagers, you do a lot of praying and worrying. You ask them to abstain, but you need to realize they're subject to human error, and leave them in the Lord's hands. My children never exhibited any behavior that led me to believe they were sexually active or doing drugs or anything really wild, but a lot of times kids can be sneaky. Sometimes it's not the fast and flirty ones you have to watch, but the innocent-looking ones you think aren't doing it.

When I was a teenager, most children were afraid to tell their parents things. You just knew most adults weren't going to be reasonable because of miscommunication or ignorance or lack of understanding. We tried to keep that line of communication open. We always told them, "If you run into trouble, tell us first. We are your friends. Trust us. We are the only ones who will stick by you through thick and thin. Nothing is too bad that you can't tell us. We're here to help you, not to hurt you." Any problem that came up, they would come to us. At least they usually did.

Children know when their parents are in earnest. There's something inside them that says, "I'm afraid to tell them, but I *have* to tell them. They deserve to know." They know what they can tell you. You don't expect them to tell you everything. They're always going to try something, if it's no more than winking at a guy. And they like to know, "You've got my back covered. You'll take care of me, no matter what." Then they don't tend to go to just anybody in the street for help. There's something in the deal for the people in the street. Nothing's free. You pay a price.

If someone gets pregnant, it's too late for punishment. That's the time to really be sensitive to the needs of the child. It's children having children. It's sad. They're having babies for you, the new grandparent, because you're the one who will take care of the babies. They're not. They don't have a job. They're not secure. And if they have a job, can they afford to take care of the baby they made? They're adding another mouth to feed and doctor bills for their family. They're putting an extra burden on the family.

I told my kids, "When you do things you know you're not supposed to do, you'll pay the price, but so will a lot of innocent people." Still, no matter who you hurt, you hurt yourself even more.

Chapter Thirty-Six

The Opposite Sex

---

*Don't let them play The Dating Game
until they're sixteen, and even then, err on
the side of caution.*

FREDA I had a strict dating rule: You had to be at least sixteen. You didn't even ask before sixteen. If you were sixteen, weekend or not, it was understood you would be home around midnight. No sixteen-year-old needs to be coming home from a date the next day, and anything after midnight is the next day.

I'm sure they do things differently now, and I know it may sound funny to some people, but nobody of the opposite sex was allowed in my children's bedrooms. It's just not appropriate for boys to be in a girl's bedroom.

If she says they want to study in her bedroom, no, no, no! I have places you can study: the dining room table, the desk, the living room, the den. The bedroom is an absolute no-no. There's no excuse for my daughter to be in her bedroom with any man except for her father or brothers. If she wants "privacy," she can shut up in the bedroom by herself. There's nothing he needs in her bedroom. He can find glasses and water and soda in the kitchen. The TV is in the den. The dining room table and desk are plenty big enough for books and studying. The bedroom and bathroom are off-limits.

They could kiss in the house. I wasn't waving a big hatchet and saying, "You can't do that." No, it's about respect—not so much respecting her father and me, but respecting herself. The young man may laugh and think it stinks at the time, but nine times out of ten, she will be the one he goes back to marry, rather than Susie, with whom he could do anything he wanted.

I was just as strict on the boys. They had no girls in their bedrooms, at least that I knew about. I never remember having to run any off. I'm sure they made jokes about me and laughed at the things I didn't see, but it's just a good thing I didn't see them.

Chapter Thirty-Seven
The Moped and the Truant

---

*Let your children know that the more
maturity and reliability they show, the more
freedom and respect they earn.*

Kimberly had her heart set on a new moped. She begged and pleaded, but her dad wouldn't budge. He wouldn't buy it. Too dangerous, he said. Freda suggested a small compromise: Kimberly could have the moped, but she'd have to pay for it herself. The moped cost $600, and she made only a dollar an hour babysitting. But the Robinsons had long ago established the importance of setting goals and working hard to achieve them, and sure enough, Kimberly worked and saved until she could buy it.

She was so proud. Like a boy with his first new car, she kept her moped garaged and cleaned and polished. She was protective of it, too, but every once in a while, she let David ride it, and he considered this a real treat. When she got her license to drive a car, she decided to give the moped to David as his birthday present.

Her mom told her David would be delighted, and he was. He rode the moped up and down the street, announcing to all his friends and neighbors it was his moped now. Oh, he thought his sister was the best in the world.

But a few months later, Kimberly met Freda in the driveway as she arrived home from work one day.

"Mama," she sobbed, "David sold the moped for $90!"

She was beside herself, both hurt and angry because her brother had virtually given away the moped she had so treasured.

"Mama, you have to get it back!" she said.

"Do you really want it?" Freda asked.

"No," Kimberly said, "but he just gave it away. I saved for that moped! I wouldn't have given it to him if I thought he didn't want it."

Freda went to David, and he said he thought he could do anything he wanted with it because it belonged to him now. He was forgetting about his sister's sentimental nature, not to mention the moped's true value.

Freda knew that the paperboy who bought the moped could have afforded to pay more and had taken advantage of David. She knew she could have gotten it back, but she also knew there was a lesson here about balancing freedom and feelings and responsibility.

"You know what?" she told David. "I am not going to ask that little boy to give the moped back. I know his mother, and I know she'd give it back. I'm going to let him keep it. But your bike is broken, and we're not going to fix it. We're not taking you anywhere, so don't ask us to drive you. From now on, you will be walking to your practices. When your $90 runs out, you're on your own."

She knew this response would make David think about what he'd done more than if she had imposed any other form of discipline. And it did. David walked around as if he were lost for days after that, and Kimberly shunned him for weeks.

From tots to teens, the Robinson children were given chores to help them develop a sense of responsibility. But in this instance, David had acted irresponsibly and betrayed his parents' and sister's respect.

Another time, Chuck betrayed his parents' trust over a more important matter, education, and Ambrose's answer was less subtle. Let's let them tell this story:

CHUCK When I was a sophomore in high school, my friends and I decided we weren't going to school one day. We all hung out at my friend Reggie's house. We had a pretty fun day and I came home—we always had to be home before my parents got home from work—and my father was in a great mood and said I could play basketball after dinner. Dumb me, I forgot if you miss school, the school calls your house to let your parents know. All the other times, I would be sure to answer the phone, and I'd hit them with a deep "Hello" and act like my father, and my parents would never know the school called. This time, I forgot the school hadn't called yet, and I was so dumb, I left and went down to my friend's house.

About 9 o'clock, my dad called and said, "I think it's time for you to come home." I didn't think anything of it and said, "Okay, I'll be right home." I got to the house and all the lights were off and I thought, "Dad just called me. The least he could have done was keep the lights on for me." I got to the door and it was locked. I thought, "Maaaan, he knew I was coming home. What's going on?" I rang the doorbell and I was still dumb. I heard him coming down the steps, and I was thinking I would ask him why he locked the door.

He opened the door and I could recognize all his different looks, and this look was like, "You lied to me." I went through my mind thinking, "Which lie did I tell?" He looked at me and said, "What did you do today?" You know how parents are. You know when they already know the answer. And I just said, "I was at Reggie's house all day."

I was a big kid now, too old to spank, but I didn't realize Dad had other ways to punish me. But to this day, I vividly remember he made his point, and made it well. He wasn't mean to me, but he straightened me out.

AMBROSE One night when I was a teenager, I sneaked out the window after we were supposed to be in bed. I was trying to chase a young lady down the street. I told my brother to let me back in when I knocked, and I trickled out. When I came back, I knocked on the window, as prearranged.

Except my dad was there, hollering, "You're not coming in here tonight!" and waving a 25-caliber gun at me.

It wasn't loaded, but I didn't know it at the time. My mother wanted to let me come in, but he wouldn't let me, and I had to sleep on the back porch all night. And it was cold and damp that night. Needless to say, I didn't do it again. It was drastic, but it worked.

CHUCK He never told me that story. No wonder he punished me! What I had pulled was stupid, and I knew it because of the way I was raised. And my children will not go undisciplined, because I know what discipline has done for me.

Part Four

College and Leaving the Nest

Chapter Thirty-Eight
Choosing the Right College

*Parents should help their children
weigh the pros and cons of each college, but
the child must make the final choice,
because interference ultimately backfires.*

Ambrose Robinson visited Virginia Military Institute and knew it was the school for David. The small campus was conducive to studying, and he liked the idea of a military school with a good engineering department. He liked the basketball coaches and dreamed that David could go straight to the pros after college, instead of spending five years in the Navy.

He was a strong-willed father and David was an obedient son, and so when Ambrose pressed for an answer, David said, "Yes, I guess I'll go to VMI." And so Ambrose called VMI, and three recruiters drove 120 miles to sign the skinny, raw recruit.

What Ambrose did not hear—or did not want to hear—was the apprehension in David's voice. His wife did, because her ears and mind were open. She had seen how awestruck David was when he came home from a weekend at the Naval Academy.

"Mom," he had said excitedly, "the equipment far exceeds any college I've been to. There is just so much more equipment. But I just can't make up my mind."

"David," she said, "I like the Naval Academy, but what do you like?"

"Dad likes VMI," he replied.

"David," she said, "go where *you* want to go, not where I want you to go or where your daddy wants you to go. Which is the best school for you?"

"The Naval Academy," David said. "Mom, you should see that lab."

What happened next depends upon whose memory is more accurate:

AMBROSE I was talking to the VMI recruiters and my wife came down the stairs saying, "*Who* are these people?"

I said, "These are the people from VMI coming to sign David."

She said, "No, they're not!"

They had driven about 120 miles and expected to sign him that day. I did, too; that's why I told them to come. David talked to his mom and David talked to me and then he told them he wasn't going to sign with them.

FREDA I met the coaches, but I didn't stay downstairs for long. Ambrose and David stayed downstairs visiting with them.

Ambrose said, "David, have you made your mind up yet?"

We didn't know he had. The coaches' ears were all up, and then David said, "I'm going to the Naval Academy," and thanked them for coming.

After they left, I said, "Did I hear you correctly? You're going to the Naval Academy? You're not going because I liked it, are you?"

He said, "Mom, it's the best place for me."

I said, "Be sure you're going there for the right reasons."

He said, "I am."

I was all happy inside, but I didn't want to start dancing, because I knew how Ambrose felt. I told him, "The education will far outweigh five years of quick money and basketball is secondary."

Ambrose didn't say much, just, "I guess you're right." He was a little disappointed. Ambrose said he always knew David would excel in basketball, and he didn't want David to tie up that option, but it all worked out. It's history after that.

DAVID My dad always thought basketball was more important to me than it really was. In his mind, pro basketball was a real option for me. In my mind, it wasn't. I think that's where we failed to communicate. To me, basketball was nothing more than something to use to get a scholarship.

AMBROSE I really felt stupid when those VMI recruiters came and Freda said no way. I was the one who called them. It was a miscommunication problem on my part. Instead of making assumptions, I should have talked with David and Freda in a three-way conversation with everyone offering their thoughts. That's how The Robinson Group functions now. Everyone has different outlooks on how things should be done. We come together as one to make decisions.

The parents should have a hand in choosing a college, but they should not force their children to go to any particular school. I went to a certain college because my dad went there and thought I should go where he went. I didn't have any problem with that, but if you make the child go to a military academy—and I think this is true seventy-five or eighty percent of the time—the child will rebel because you made him suffer all this pain. He'll think, "I'm going to stay here for five months, make my parents happy, and then I'm getting out."

So I don't think you should *make* children go to a particular school. I used the power of persuasion only to point out what I thought were the positives and negatives of a school. For instance, my wife and I knew Chuck wanted to go to a college away from home just to meet a lot of girls. We thought that was the wrong reason to accept a scholarship, and we discouraged him. He was going to major in something ridiculous such as basket weaving, if you will. I gave him the pros and cons as I saw them, but I did not say, "You can't go." Instead, I said, "This is not the place for you," and I probably said it in a tone that he figured meant no. I have a way of saying something and it's pretty obvious what I mean.

151

I thought a military academy was the best place for David and Chuck. The first year there, you become a man. By the time you graduate, you can handle just about anything that comes up. But a lot of the students who go to an academy because someone else wants them to end up dropping out in their first or second year. So it's extremely important they make a college choice without any coercion from their parents. Guidance, yes. Coercion, no.

CHUCK One time when I was in ninth grade we were driving in the car and my father told me, "You know, you'll have to get a scholarship, because we can't afford to send you to college." I took it pretty serious, because he didn't joke very often. Nothing else was said, but I always remembered that. I didn't know how I could go to college on a scholarship, but I knew I had to do it.

So, once I was a senior, I knew I had to concentrate on one sport and try to get a scholarship. I still ran track, but I concentrated on basketball. I never thought I was that good in basketball. I took it the same way I took my grades. Growing up in my household, average was not enough. I played a little above average on the basketball court, but it didn't seem like enough. Remember, when I was a senior in high school, I had a brother who had just been drafted No. 1 in the NBA draft. I averaged twenty-two or twenty-four points a game in high school, which was nothing, but it got me a scholarship.

As a high school senior, I looked forward to visiting colleges, but when I actually started doing it, it was terrible. It was a big burden on my mind. I told James Madison I would come and play for Lefty Driesell. My mind was pretty much made up. I've always been organized. I kept a journal and laid out all the pros and cons of each school, giving them marks and checks and stars. I applied to the Naval Academy only because my mother told me to apply. I never thought I was smart enough to get in. I got my packet in late, and so a week before I was to leave to go to James Madison, I got my acceptance letter from the Naval Academy. I wrote in my journal, "Oh darn. This is a big wrench in my plans. Now I've got to make a choice." I really wasn't looking that forward to going, but I thought, "I'll try it out. I'll go for a while and see if I like it."

FREDA Chuck fooled all of us. He was *the* laid-back kid. He told me when he graduated from high school he wanted a bicycle. I said to Kim, "What in the world would he want a bicycle for?" She said, "Mom, don't buy it for him. He told me he wanted it so he could ride around campus and check the women out." I said, "Well, thank you. He will not be getting a bicycle."

He took his time picking a college. Two or three schools were pursuing him for basketball. Chuck took the SAT again, and the Naval Academy wanted him to come, but he didn't act interested. So I said, "Chuck, you're going to go to school. You're going to work or go to school or go in the service. You're not going to idle around and get into trouble. You're going to do something."

Three weeks before colleges were to open, he came to us and said he had called the Naval Academy and accepted his appointment. We couldn't believe it. We were surprised but really pleased because he needed this discipline. I said to myself, "Thank you, Lord," but I didn't dare breathe it out loud.

KIMBERLY We grew up in a household where the expectation is you either go to college or you get a job. College was a given. My father told me, "If you don't go to college, the military will give you a secure job." To me, that was not an option. I visited one of my friends at Howard for a weekend and thought, "Oh, wow, I really like this school." It was a black college, and I wanted to get some experience with my own culture. We had grown up in white areas. We were always the ones who stood out (as minorities) in the community events. When I went to Howard that weekend, I got to be around people like me.

My father wanted me to go to one of the in-state schools because they were cheaper, but I was creative in getting grants and making money. My first year, my parents didn't pay one dime. I would estimate they paid less than $2,000 for my whole college career.

Chapter Thirty-Nine

Newfound Independence

Parents need to teach children how to live on their own before they leave the nest—but then they must back away and let their youngsters spread their wings.

Learning to juggle studies and parties, homework and house-work is a crash course in independence and self-sufficiency. If students don't enter college with enough maturity and life skills, they can flunk out fast.

Even amid Navy's highly structured routine, many students didn't have the discipline and motivation to study without mom and dad looking over their shoulders. Even David, despite all the discipline he had learned at home, leaned toward lackadaisical.

This is not good when your courses include thermodynamics, navigation, advanced calculus, physics, computer science, electrical engineering, weapons, history of science and technology, contemporary American literature, advanced programming, celestial navigation, advanced numerical analysis, computer data structures, partial differential equation, and economic geography.

David said homework came in two forms: too much and way too much.

DAVID I really had to be pushed to achieve. My mother did the pushing. My father was the enforcer. But sometimes you need prodding from outside your family, too. You only listen to so much your parents tell you. When you get it from other sources, that has an effect on you, too. When I got to the Naval Academy, they changed me from a person who did enough to get by and be successful, into a person who really wanted to excel. The discipline I learned at the Naval Academy made it easier to do all the things I do now.

AMBROSE David will tell you to this day he went to the Academy because of the academics and the discipline. It's a different type of discipline than what he had at home. He needed that discipline to study. He didn't study the way I thought he should. He will tell you today he didn't study at all. Chuck was the same way. I was the same way. David didn't study as much as he should have his last two years in high school and his first year in college. He could skate and still make a B. But I didn't want my kids to make the mistakes I made. That's why David got restricted when he got a C; I knew he could do better.

He couldn't skate at the Academy. You know what the load was? His first semester, David validated two classes and still took nineteen hours. Add in marching and basketball practice and traveling with the team, and that's a heavy load. His first year, he just barely got through. During class, David would sleep, and would sleep virtually any way he could—standing, sitting, you name it. At first Navy thought he had some sort of a medical problem, but we found out he was constantly tired because he was growing so fast. He didn't put that much effort into studying that first year, and his academics suffered. His grade point average was barely passing. Then he realized, "Maybe I better get off my tail and start working," and eventually he raised his average to a 3.2.

FREDA They're thrown straight into independent decision-making. They leave the nest and they're flying inde-

155

pendently, out on their own. They're a little weak, and you pray they will be strengthened, because they're not on your wings anymore. You pray they make the right decisions and pray the Lord takes care of them. If you've instilled the right values, you shouldn't worry too much, because the groundwork's been laid. That's why it's so important to build a solid foundation while they're young.

The best thing you can do is communicate with them on the phone and visit when you can. Always tell them, "If you have questions, call us. We will always be there to help you. Don't hide things from us or keep things inside. Stress is the last thing you need. Talk to us, and if we don't know how to help, we can find somebody to help. If you need a tutor, tell us and we will find one. If you need help, don't wait until you flunk to tell us you're in trouble. You need to tell us before something happens." We stressed prevention.

They want and need their independence. When we made surprise visits to campus, we'd see them walking and they'd look at us and say, "Did you want something?" And we'd say, "No, we just wanted to holler at you." Another time we'd be on the phone with them and say, "Did you do so and so?" And they'd say, "Mom, I've done that already. I've been doing it a while, remember?" You have to smile and keep going. You have to consciously back off.

If they didn't learn how to cook or clean or do laundry before they went to college, they will need a crash course now. We tried to make sure they didn't need one. We can teach them all day long, but we can't teach them how to deal with every problem they'll meet. They have to get out there and roll up their sleeves and attack problems head on. We can tell them all day long it's cold and snowing, but they don't know that for sure until they get outside. They need the experiences. That's a part of growing. That's called continued growth.

AMBROSE The load of course work was more than they were used to. Plebe year is really tough. It teaches you to be a man, to accept responsibility and do things in the face of

156

adversity. We'd tell them, "This is the background that will prepare you for the rest of your life. Today is the beginning of the rest of your life." I tried to show my children the light at the end of the tunnel, because I knew they'd work toward it better than if I didn't explain why it was important. They had a reason to do well. They were expected to do well.

I'd make suggestions, and I'm sure sometimes they'd go in one ear and out the other. But as a parent, you have to try. Look at the people who pay for advice: Even presidents need advice. Who better to give advice than parents? Some of our advice might be old-fashioned, but there's a reason why old-fashioned advice endures. It works.

Chapter Forty
Stay or Go?

Parents must shift from running their children's lives to guiding them and counseling them on their college choices.

David Robinson will never forget his first day at the Naval Academy.

"The longest day ever," he calls it.

In the morning, he got sworn in.

In the evening, he got swore at.

All day and all night, he got bossed around like a common criminal.

"What have I gotten myself into?" he asked himself, and sleep did not come easy that night.

And then he was required to swim one hundred meters. Four laps. He couldn't make it.

"I thought about quitting," he says. "It was the only time I thought about quitting."

That is to be expected. Whether it's a simple case of homesickness those first few weeks or something more serious, just about every student at a new college at some point ponders quitting or changing schools.

When their "babies" head off to college, parents, especially mothers, deal with intense loneliness.

Their children's loneliness. Their own loneliness.

When David and Chuck were homesick and overworked, their parents reassured them. But when Kimberly told Ambrose she wanted to drop out for a semester, he called her a quitter, because he was afraid she wouldn't go back.

When David grew from 6'7½" upon acceptance to Navy to a strapping 7 feet by the end of his sophomore year and blossomed from good high school player to college star and pro prospect, his choice was difficult. He could transfer before classes began his third year, owe no military commitment and find a school that might better prepare him for the NBA's rigors and riches. Or he could take his chances with Navy officials, who suggested they might not hold him to the full commitment but offered nothing in writing.

FREDA I missed Kim, but I did have the two boys left, so I didn't cry the day she left for college. I cried for Chuck, because he was the last one to leave, and I felt alone. The house felt so empty. But the best thing to do is cry and get it over with, to release the tension. When your kids leave, you get lonesome from time to time, but it never lasts too long. You're always glad to hear their voices on the phone, even if they're calling collect. I guarantee this: You'll never say, "I won't accept the charges."

AMBROSE David called home all the time that first year, and Chuck called a lot, too. Crazy boys—always called collect. We helped them get over their depressions. Every child gets homesick at first. You help them resolve their homesickness. You're their sounding board.

Chuck caught hell his first year at Navy. Everyone compared him to David. But Chuck did better at Navy than some of those high school valedictorians.

CHUCK You're not supposed to like the first weeks there, but I hated it even more than most. They got on me more because of who I was. The whole first year I called home and told my mom how much I hated it. I hated that school with a passion.

159

Most moms, if you call them up and tell them how much you hate it and all the things they did wrong to you, will say, "I'm calling so and so and you can come home right now." Others tell you, "Stick it out. Just stick it out." My mom would say, "There's a room for you at the house if you ever want to come home," and she'd leave it at that. She never told me to stay there, never told me I had to graduate. She just left it up to me. For about a year that went on, and then, even though I still hated it, I didn't whine when I called home anymore.

I got through that and ended up having *the* best time in college. Out of all the people who've ever gone to the Naval Academy, I'm sure I had *the* best time. I can say it now—well, I probably shouldn't say it—but I broke every rule there was to break. It was like a ritual for me. If I didn't break a rule that day, I felt bad. Because I figured, "They're putting me through so much here, I've got to break at least one rule today." It might just mean stepping out in the hall after midnight because you weren't supposed to come out of your room after 12, but I had a blast.

That's not to say I liked the actual school. I love what the education did for me, but you're not supposed to really like school. The day to day was not for me. I've never been a very military person.

At the Naval Academy, when you break rules, you get demerits and get put on restriction. If you're a freshman, they make you march on Saturdays. If you're an upperclassman, you get put on restriction for, say, two weeks or a month, depending on how severe the infraction was.

My mom will tell you I was great at breaking rules and getting away with it. I figured if I did get caught, the punishment could not possibly equal all the dirt I'd done. I only got caught two times. I got in trouble right before my senior year and was put on restriction for a week or so. As a freshman, I got in trouble once for telling the truth. All the freshmen were supposed to go see a boat one Saturday. I don't know if I forgot or what the reason was, but I didn't go. School had just started maybe two weeks before. They asked who didn't go see the boat, and I knew half of us didn't go see it. But my dumb roommate and I

160

raised our hands. We had to march for six hours on a Saturday because we told on ourselves. From then on, I didn't offer up any information.

AMBROSE David, Freda, and I discussed at length the pros and cons of staying at Navy versus transferring to a basketball factory. But if David transferred, he'd have to sit out his first year, and there was no guarantee he'd play even then. He was concerned about going to a basketball school where, knowing his talents were not fully developed, he could and probably would be relegated to the bench in a backup role. He remembers thinking, "Where would I go? Would I be comfortable? Would I play center? What if I transfer somewhere and then a hotshot shows up?"

David and I eventually had meetings with the Naval Academy superintendent to determine what if anything could be done. Obviously, Navy wanted to keep him, and obviously, David was comfortable at Navy, but he had to consider other options. We clearly understood that at the end of his senior year, he could request he not be commissioned because he was too tall. The Navy officials indicated they'd show some flexibility; if they hadn't, we might have decided differently. So we made a decision jointly to keep David at Navy rather than have him sit out a year and lose that development, because, as he has said, in five years, he'd still be 7'1". We chose academics ahead of basketball. David showed his loyalty to the Navy and was praised for choosing to serve his country instead of letting the almighty dollar rule his life.

We were hoping they'd let him have a two-year commitment and play pro basketball at the same time, the way they were letting Napoleon McCallum play pro football in his spare time. Ultimately, they decided that, because he was too tall to serve at sea, David's commitment would be reduced from five years to two years, but that he couldn't play ball during that time. They let other servicemen out for lesser problems, but David was so high profile, they couldn't do it for fear of public backlash and of making the exception become the rule.

I feel they were trying to show future students they wouldn't be let out to go pro. They ended up making an example of Napoleon McCallum, too. They changed the rule that allowed him to play football on active duty and transferred him to an area where it was impossible for him to play with his team. I think the Navy thought he was getting too much attention, but I disagree. That was free advertisement for the Navy, the kind of media attention that is invaluable for the military.

DAVID When we made that decision, my parents played the same role they'd always played. They wouldn't give me their opinions directly, but every time I asked them about certain possibilities, they were glad to help me. But they wanted me to make the decision. We talked many times over the course of the next few months. I knew long before I had to make the decision that other schools would be interested in me. It was just a matter of deciding what was my best option. The long-term security of graduating from the Naval Academy was the worst-bet scenario and the best-bet scenario was I'd still be playing in the pros five years after graduating. I saw the worst-bet scenario and the upside. If I went to another school, the worst-bet scenario didn't seem so great. In retrospect, it was a great decision.

AMBROSE Now, back in '83, '84, my daughter really challenged us. She had maybe a semester and a half left, and she got tired and didn't want to go back to college. I told her, "Okay, if you quit, you know you'll never be anything. You'll never finish college." She says today that instilled in her a sense of pride. She would show me she could get her education. And she did.

My dad said the same thing to me when I got kicked out of college, and it made me think, "Well, I'll just show you." And that's exactly what happened. I got kicked out in December of '60 and I joined the Navy in January of '61, and I rose to the second-highest rank an enlisted man can achieve. But it was '77 before I got my degree. She was the oldest and I wanted to see her get her degree. It hurt me. I didn't believe she'd only quit for a semester. I thought school was too much a struggle for her and she had given up. Hence some of the words I used.

FREDA Kim was having trouble grasping statistics. She said she couldn't take it anymore. She said, "I need a rest or I think I'm going to lose it. I promise you, I'll go back next semester." I didn't want her to feel compelled to stay in school and then have a breakdown. She was frustrated and disillusioned. I felt maybe she needed a break, and even if she didn't go back to school, it wasn't the end of the world. Her father didn't come right out and call her a quitter, but he implied it, and that upset me. I thought Ambrose's approach was cruel. This is a prime example of parents making mistakes while learning with their children.

AMBROSE It might have been cruel, but she'll tell you to this day, that's probably what motivated her to do what she's doing.

FREDA It could have motivated her, because when I followed her downstairs afterward, she was crying and told me, "I *will* show him. I'll finish if it's the last thing I do." And that she did. But I think Ambrose should have given her the benefit of the doubt. Sometimes you really can make a person feel like a quitter.

AMBROSE There are some things I look back on that I might handle differently today and that's one of them. If I had it to do over again, I'd try to help her with her schoolwork, rather than just let her struggle. But if she said she wanted to quit, I'd probably say the same thing again.

KIMBERLY I never wanted to drop out. I just wanted to take a semester off. But they were concerned that I wouldn't go back. That wasn't the case. I was having a hard time. I was working, paying for college myself, and it was a struggle.

163

I told my dad I was $900 short for the next semester. He said, "You better start working full time." I won't tell you what I thought. Yes, I said I'd show him, but that was just part of my vocabulary. Whatever I asked was so little to consider, I thought it shouldn't even be an issue. I had paid for almost all of college myself. I thought, "With everything I'm doing, can't you let this go?" I viewed it as a direct slap. Two days later, I found a check on my bed for the $900.

AMBROSE I'm proud of her, too. She's going to become the first doctor in our immediate family.

Chapter Forty-One

A Star is Born

*Do not sacrifice education by overem-
phasizing sports, and do not interfere with
the coaches.*

Good Morning America showed up in Annapolis, Maryland, one day to talk about life at the Naval Academy. The hosts
spoke with the Navy's most famous lieutenant and plebe, David
Robinson and brother Chuck, and glorified the importance of a
Navy education.

But the lead sports story in the D.C. area that day leaned to
the opposite extreme: Dexter Manley, the Washington Redskins'
star pass rusher, had tested positive for drugs for a third time
and faced a lifetime suspension. He was admitted to college and
had played four years of college football—even though he could
barely read. He left college ill-prepared for the fast-paced world
of football, fame, and fortune, and he had fallen prey.

Manley is not alone. Scads of athletes have succumbed to
society's ills and sports' lure and lucre. Steep odds face every
college athlete who dreams of the pros. We all know what happens when an athlete spends all his time on balls and not books,
and we decry them as fools. Yet when it is our son who is the
athlete, we get so caught up in the excitement and hoopla and
reflected glory, we rationalize that he will be the exception.

165

So, even in college, it's important to make sports just one part of a full life. Let's remember that making the pros is a million-to-one shot. Let's remember Chuck Robinson, the more accomplished high school athlete, is the rule and David Robinson, the sudden 7-footer, is the exception. If an athlete has a true shot at the pros, sure, he should work hard to reach his potential, and chances are, he'll have to work harder than David did. But he should never forget about academics, because even if he makes the pros, what does he do when he gets hurt, when he is fired or retired?

Ambrose and Freda Robinson addressed these issues early on, and because David never even envisioned a pro career until he was at least a sophomore or junior, keeping sports in perspective might not have been as hard for him as it is for other athletes. "I didn't care whether I played basketball at the Academy. I just wanted to get good grades and fit in," he says.

That wasn't always easy, because basketball was not a game but an occupation for his bosses. Navy coaches didn't get many players of David's size and athletic ability. Because of the tight confines in Navy ships, students weren't supposed to be taller than 6'6", though as many as five percent could be admitted as tall as 6'8". David barely fit that upper limit when he took his physical in February. He was 6'7½]"—and 6'9" when he began orientation in May. But for that quirk in growth spurts, who knows how his story would have turned out?

But once Paul Evans signed him, the hard-driving coach demanded total dedication. David didn't share that enthusiasm. "It was obvious that basketball was not real important to him and there wasn't much he liked about it that year, including practice," recalls Pete Herrmann, Evans' assistant for David's first three years and the head coach for David's senior year. "He told me he would sit in his math class sixth period and say to himself, 'Oh, brother I have to go to basketball practice today.' It's a strange way to begin an All-American career."

The Middies hadn't had an All-American since 1933, hadn't qualified for the NCAA tournament since 1966, but with David growing and the coaches prodding, the turnaround began. Playing part-time as a 6'9", 185-pound freshman string bean, his numbers were modest—7.6 points, 4.0 rebounds, and 1.3 blocks per game—but David was named ECAC South Rookie of the Year, Navy won twenty games for the first time in history, and both were on their way.

David began lifting weights and playing in the rugged Washington, D.C. summer leagues, and returned as a sophomore as a 6'11", 215-pound starter. He led Navy to a 26–6 record and got a trip to the NCAAs by averaging 23.6 points, 11.6 rebounds, and 4.0 blocks a game. He started thinking he might have a shot at the pros, but still, he told his dad, "Basketball is just something else to do, one facet of life."

He wasn't close to realizing his potential, and Evans tried to motivate him by screaming at him and even throwing him out of practice at times. Evans chewed on him more than a dollar steak, but David didn't respond the way the coach expected. "Paul Evans is a little like Bobby Knight," he once told ESPN. "It was important to me to tune a little of that out and motivate myself." He even threatened to quit the team. "I was just trying to enjoy myself," he told GQ. "Evans was playing these mind games to motivate me. Yelling at me to get me mad. That may work with some guys, but not me. I just got mad at him. I told him, 'Hey, man, you're being a jerk. Just tell me what you want me to do.' Eventually we stopped communicating." But the team didn't stop winning until they faced top-ranked Duke one game before the Final Four. David averaged 22.7 points, led the nation with 13.0 rebounds and 5.9 blocks a game, and set NCAA records for blocks in a game, season, and career. He was named an All-American by just about every organization save The Associated Press and United Press International.

Herrmann took over when Evans left for the University of Pittsburgh, and "allowed me to be myself, so I worked harder," said David, who was even better as a senior. He led the nation again in blocked shots and ranked third in scoring and fourth in rebounding. He became the first college player to combine 2,500 points with 1,300 rebounds and sixty percent shooting from the floor. He made every All-American team and all the major College Player of the Year awards. He set thirty-three Navy records, launched the Midshipmen to another NCAA play-off appearance, and closed with a career-high fifty points.

But even though he was working harder and achieving more in basketball, he didn't forget about the rest of his life. He balanced studies, sports, coaches, and media obligations with equal aplomb. "David Robinson was a joy to be around," Herrmann said. "He handled the media attention the way you'd want your own son to handle it. It's a credit to him and his family that he always maintained his composure."

The Robinson family maintained their composure even in the rare sour times. They did not scream when a new Secretary of the Navy overturned his predecessor's position and said David could not play part-time in the NBA during his two-year military commitment. They stayed quiet when David was misused by 1988 Olympics coach John Thompson and, despite a year off from competitive action, was criticized when what was supposed to be another automatic gold medal turned to bronze.

AMBROSE I never complained to any coach, not even to John Thompson. I strongly disagreed with his approach, but I still didn't say anything to him. It's not the parents' place.

So many parents these days tell the coach, "You've got to play my child." Well, the coach knows what he's doing. We've had several incidents here in San Antonio with parents interfering with high school coaches. It's not right. There were times I wanted to say something, but I never did, even when I saw things that were obviously wrong. I saw several times his first year at Navy when he should have been playing and wasn't, but I never said anything.

I liked David's high school coach, Art Payne. He was a great guy. He knew David didn't know that much about basketball. I didn't interfere, though, and he'd come to me and ask how to deal with David. Paul Evans did, too, that first year at Navy. I couldn't always answer him; I didn't know what was going on in David's head. Paul would ask, "What can I do to get this guy going?" I told him I didn't know, and I was being honest. I did know David didn't like Paul yelling at him, but sometimes that probably did prod him on. David did some things just to show Paul he could do them.

I had a good rapport with the Navy coaches. I would drive the sixty or so miles every opportunity I could. I drove a 1979 Pontiac Bonneville with the license plate NA50VY to indicate my son played for Navy, his position was center, and his number was fifty. I would attend practices and once the season started, all the games within two hundred miles of my home. Occasionally, I would even drive to North Carolina. Over four years, I put more than eighty thousand miles on that car, mostly associated with basketball.

I still don't interfere with what the coaches are doing now in San Antonio. That's how I maintain my rapport with all of them. I don't tell them what to do. That's not my job.

Chapter Forty-Two
Racial Awakening

Once they're mature enough to handle it, children should learn about racism and how to cope with it.

David Robinson was sixteen when he lost his racial innocence.

The party was just down the street, thrown by the daughter of a naval warrant officer. Everybody there was white, save David, but he thought nothing of it until they decided to play Spin the Bottle.

The teens gathered 'round and suddenly, there was this awkward hesitation; the white kids glanced at David and whispered among each other—and then asked him to "referee."

Sheltered by his parents and growing up in more serene neighborhoods and times, he hadn't confronted issues of race. He had lived in mostly white neighborhoods, but was gifted enough athletically, academically, and socially that he rarely felt slighted.

"I was always in the gifted classes with whites," he says. "It never dawned on me I was black. And a black kid can only go so far. As much as you want to believe everyone is so equal, you know when it comes down to kissing somebody or whatever, a line is drawn. That was a harsh reality. Everybody was saying, 'Oh, Dave, you're so great, such a nice guy,' but it comes down to playing Spin the Bottle and they look at you funny like, 'Is *he* going to play?' And then you start to feel, 'Look at me. I'm different in their eyes.' And that's a hard lesson.

"It made me realize that wasn't really my place. I was with them a lot of time—I never thought of myself as not being one of them—but they weren't my people. That shocks you a little bit. I'd never spent a lot of time around blacks, so socially, I was kind of backward. I didn't know where I belonged. It was hard for me to hang with other blacks. I felt out of place. I realized I was black; I certainly couldn't pretend I was white. I just didn't know how to *be* black. I had to work at it."

He joined black clubs in college to work at it, but race was still a minor enough issue in his life that he and his family were surprised and hurt when, despite all his accomplishments, his Navy teammates spurned David and chose a white teammate as their captain his senior season.

His full awakening came a few months later, when he began his military duty in Kings Bay, Georgia, and adopted a Little Brother in a poor black section of town. There, he saw poverty in education, income, and opportunity. There, he saw drug addicts, prostitutes, teenaged mothers, and dreams dashed by a century of discrimination.

"I was afraid to park my car at that little boy's house," he says. "It was all so sad. There was no hope, no ambition. I was scared to death. It was real life. I had always been judged on my abilities, never on whether I was black or white. I had been sheltered. I realized what a privileged life I had. I got on my knees and asked God to show me a way I could give back some of my blessings."

Rude racist realities also hit Kimberly when she chose to attend a black college.

KIMBERLY Out of 760 people in my high school class, fifty-eight of us were black. When I got to college, I found the white schools weren't teaching me real history; they were teaching me what they wanted me to know. The only things the white schools taught me about black people was that we were

171

once in slavery, and that Martin Luther King had fought for blacks, and then he died. I didn't learn the intricacies. What I knew about black history didn't scratch the surface.

At Howard, I learned exactly how we were brought into slavery: how we got here; how we were put on that boat; how we were stacked on top of each other and shackled and couldn't move, even if it meant doing a bodily function on top of someone else. We were taken from our native country and used here in slavery, sold to make money, then forced to serve as free labor. Then masters raped their slaves and mulattos were born. We were given the last names of the masters. They didn't want us to educate ourselves. They wanted us to remain blind, and even after we were "free," they didn't let us vote. Even after slavery, we were kept beneath what was considered civilization. It reminded me of giants stepping on ants.

It was definitely an eye-opening experience. I was really mad. A lot of episodes from my past finally clicked. Like when the kids played Spin the Bottle and said, "David, you be the bottle spinner."

When I told my parents I was learning about racism, they told me, "I know that. I've been there."

I asked, "Why didn't you tell me? I'm just learning this now? I'm learning it too late! All these years, they've been treating us like this and I'm just finding out?"

My mother said I came back a militant after my first semester. She said, "Kim, you can't be like that."

I agree with her. You don't want to raise a kid to be militant or violent. That first semester I was revved up and accusing everybody. I was reading racism into everything. But it was just that one semester. After that, I didn't let it get to me anymore.

One time during college I was working in a Safeway store and a man came up and threw a steak on the counter and said, "Ring it up, nigger." And there were other people in line! It wasn't like nobody else heard it.

One time after he was out of the military, David and I went to Quantico to the golf course and snack bar, and when we sat down, the lady said, "We're not serving anybody else." We said all we wanted was a sandwich or soda. She said, huffily, "Sorry, we're not serving anybody else." We said, "What about those two people? You're serving them." She just said, "Sorry." It was apparent she wasn't helping us because we were black.

This is today's society. What can you do? Someone calls you nigger, what can you do? Say a prayer for the person, that's all. I don't have time for that stuff. I was in church one day and someone said, "The Bible says turn the other cheek. But if someone's hitting me upside the head, I'm going to run out of cheeks." Hey, it's not worth the aggravation. Especially the mild incidents.

Now, all of a sudden on the news, everything is about race. But it didn't just happen. It's gone on for years. It's just subtler. Racism isn't always an attack. It could be monetary action, social, work action. It's still prevalent. I don't think it will go away. Sure, I have hope, but I'm also realistic. You can pray about it, you can actively work not to promote it, but you can't just put a Band-Aid on it. We have so many anti-Semitic groups, so many hate groups. All you can do is say a prayer and hope. Sometimes you can't help but wonder what it will be like for your children.

CHUCK I was fortunate to grow up in integrated neighborhoods. I had every race of friend you could think of, whereas my brother and sister grew up in predominantly white neighborhoods, so at times they were a little estranged from their race. I had white friends and I had black friends, and it didn't matter to me as long as they were fun to be around. I never faced any overt racial issues as a child.

I've faced more racism in Mississippi since I've been out of college than anywhere else. They may not call you names, but it's still overt. It's sad.

I've been pulled over by the cops probably a total of twenty times since I was in college and have never gotten a ticket. Sometimes they've pulled me over because I was speeding or doing something wrong, but I'd say out of the twenty times, at least thirteen were just because I was a black man driving a nice car.

173

When I first got my Lexus, I had thirty-day tags on it. I pulled onto the highway and saw a cop behind me. When you see a cop behind you, you make sure you do everything right, but less than a mile later, he pulled me over. He saw me and a brother from my church—two black guys in Mississippi—and said, "Is this your car?"

I said, "Yes. I've got thirty-day tags because I just bought it."

He checked everything and said, "I was just checking."

I'm not positive that wouldn't happen to a white guy, but it's happened to me enough times that I can say with confidence there is less chance of it happening to a white person.

When I got my Porsche, I was in Virginia and was pulled over about 8 o'clock at night. A cop was driving slow, about thirty in a forty-mph speed limit, so I passed him. He pulled me over and said, "Is this your father's car you're driving, son?" And I said, "No sir." He asked for all my paperwork and I gave it to him and he checked it out and gave it back and never said why he pulled me over.

I was out one night in San Antonio, walking around my parents' neighborhood, and I noticed the security guard driving by me a bunch of times in little circles. I thought, "There's got to be more than one street in Elm Creek." Finally he stopped and asked if I lived there, and I told him yes and gave him the address.

It's the way of the world. I say that's the way it is and the way it will always be, because that's what the Bible says. The Bible says there's nothing new under the sun. All you personally can do is live right and be fair. It really doesn't bother me, because I know people don't know any better. They're ignorant. I have no problem not eating at a certain restaurant because someone doesn't like my race. I have no problem going to a different place; there's plenty of places that will take my money. That's how I look at it.

I don't expect much from people. Because if you expect a lot from people, you will always be disappointed. So when I meet people and they prove to be great, that's a blessing. That's a bonus.

FREDA I've seen policemen not charge a white boy because they say, "I know his daddy." But they'll charge the black boy. They stop you in your pretty car, like they harassed David once in Virginia, and ask, "Boy, where you get this car from? Whose car is this?"

David was in the car with his future wife, and the cop said, "This ain't your car. It must be your daddy's car. What does he do?" Then he looked at David's license and said, "Well, I stopped you because you were wobbling down the road." But David doesn't drink, and he wasn't sleepy. David had already graduated from the Academy, he was stationed in Georgia, and he was home for Christmas, visiting with his fiancee, and this was the treatment he got for serving his country.

We've had all sorts of unpleasant, bad experiences, but we always managed to rise above them. I call it "Welcome to America."

CHUCK My mom went to the golf course once looking for David and they told her, "The cooks don't work today." I probably would have said, "He could buy this place, let alone cook for this place." So that's a perfect example. Regardless of what level you're at, whether you're middle class or whatever, it can happen to you if you're black.

Part Five

Building an
MVP Life and Career

Chapter Forty-Three

Starting Anew

───────

*Parents can help children sort out the
choices for careers, employers, and homes.*

After four years of classes and clashes, revelry and rivalry,
study and sweat, the graduates accept their diplomas and congratulations and throw their caps into the air.

"I was definitely proud when that moment came," Ambrose
says. "It made me feel so good when Kim got her master's, and
I'll be all smiles, cheesing and grinning and everything else,
when she gets her doctorate."

It is the end of one era and the start of another.

Or, as David inscribed under his photo in the Naval Academy's 1987 yearbook: "Let it be known that I had fun and made
some great friends. I braved many new experiences and traveled to many countries. I went from a 'swizzle stick in a blender'
to a 'senior All-American.' Now, though, it's time to move on."

Time to move on to their careers.

For most graduates, that means starting at the bottom,
working their way up, and hoping they can choose from among
a few five-figure job offers.

David's options were a tad better.

Three days after he graduated from the Naval Academy
and was assigned to Kings Bay, Georgia, the San Antonio Spurs

won the NBA draft lottery and promptly announced they would select David No. 1 despite his Navy commitment.

Most athletes have little choice but to sign with the team that drafts them. But because David was already making money, albeit modest, and could not play for two years anyway, he had other options. He could sign with the Spurs, or wait until the 1988 draft and let someone else pick him. If he didn't like the second team, he could spurn its offer, and, just when his Naval duty ended, he could be free to sign with anyone. He could pick his favorite city, team, and contract after what figured to be an all-out bidding war for one of those "franchise" centers who arrive maybe once or twice a decade.

Even in the multi-million dollar world of the NBA, this was leverage players only dreamt of. After the Spurs drafted David No. 1 in June and his parents and cousin helped him screen and select Lee Fentress of Advantage International as his agent, the Robinsons were decidedly noncommittal. San Antonio would have to prove it wanted them, and so the Spurs and the city set about doing that.

David spent the summer playing in the Pan Am Games and working as a civil engineer in charge of construction at Kings Bay's explosive handling wharf, the pier from which nuclear missiles would be loaded aboard Trident subs.

It was in September that he made his first visit to San Antonio, and the greeting was something out of a storybook.

San Antonio was one of the nation's largest cities, but outside the city limits, the people practically vanished. It was a small metropolitan and television market by pro sports standards, and the Spurs were the only pro sport in town. In Los Angeles, with its many pro and college teams and beaches and diversions, the Lakers were but one entertainment outlet. In San Antonio, the Spurs meant everything to sports fans and everything to the big-league image the city was trying to build. The mayor wanted to build a domed stadium in hopes of keeping the Spurs and luring an NFL franchise, but the prospects were dismal unless "The Admiral" landed. The Spurs weren't winning, they weren't drawing good crowds, and they wouldn't be staying in San Antonio much longer if they didn't turn around in a hurry.

John Paul II visited the city the week before, but Spurs majority owner Angelo Drossos claimed his seven-foot savior was "more important to San Antonio than the Pope. Hopefully, he will lead us to the Promised Land."

David didn't want a royal greeting, but with so much at stake, how could San Antonio help but proceed with pomp and circumstance?

The Spurs spent $16,000 just to charter a private jet that would pick up Ambrose, Freda, and Chuck Robinson and two agents in Washington, D.C., ferry them to Jacksonville, Florida, to pick up David, and take them to San Antonio.

Upon landing, the Robinsons and the two agents were greeted by seven hundred screaming fans, the Chamber of Commerce Red Carpet Welcoming Committee, and the DeCampanis Mariachi Band. Rain was forecast, but as if by omen, the skies turned blue and the sun prevailed just as they disembarked. As they trod across the red carpet, the band played "Anchors Aweigh." The fans chanted "David! David! David!" and waved signs with messages such as "Say Yes, David" and "Pretty Please." A state senator made "The Admiral" an honorary admiral in the Texas State Navy. David said a few words to the fans, retreated inside to talk with the media—he wore a Lakers purple T-shirt as he told them he would keep an open mind—and then a limousine whisked them to their hotel suites.

Spurs management and players feted the Robinsons over dinner and a nightclub tour that night, and the next morning, they were given a helicopter tour of the city by none other than the mayor, Henry Cisneros. "We've done everything we could except widen the San Antonio River to bring in a battleship," said Cisneros, who would go on to serve in President Clinton's Cabinet as Secretary of Housing and Urban Development. After lunch and golf at the city's poshest country club, the Dominion, they had a private dinner at a fancy French restaurant and a riverboat ride along the city's famed Riverwalk. They met with

Spurs management the following day and flew home, making no promises, saying only that they would remain open-minded.

FREDA When we got into San Antonio, we played a little joke on them. We didn't let David get off the plane right away. Everybody got off the plane, and Chuck got off the plane behind us, and they thought they had gotten ripped off. Then after a little pause, David got off the plane, and they went off! The weekend began right there, a real class weekend. They put us up in a really nice hotel, in big suites, the biggest suite I'd ever been in. I had a bedroom, a dining room, and a living room with a fireplace. We had flowers and a wet bar with the counter covered with jumbo shrimp. It was dreamland. The festivities continued the whole weekend. We went to a reception party that night, and the next morning, the mayor and one of the local developers gave us a tour of the city in two helicopters. It was the best tour I'd ever had, just gorgeous. We landed on the Dominion grounds for dinner, and the helicopter sat there until we were ready to leave.

Since we were just regular middle-class people, this was a real treat. You pinch yourself and say, "Thank God." Whoever put that weekend together deserves a medal. It was first class all the way. But while we appreciated the hospitality, you can't judge a place on just one weekend.

AMBROSE I had no idea what San Antonio was all about when the Spurs drafted David. All I could think of were the old cowboy movies and tumbleweeds and prairie grass. So when we came here, the first thing that impressed me was all the greenery. Then all the hoopla. It left a good impression. Management wanted us. The whole city supported us.

David had a lot of options. We evaluated everything. He could go to the Lakers or Celtics, but might wind up playing behind Kareem Abdul-Jabbar or Robert Parish for a couple of years. I guess it was thought it would take a center two years or more to develop. We looked at the salary caps, and most of the best teams couldn't afford what David's agents were looking for.

182

One factor that helped us make our decision was that San Antonio reminded David of Navy. He saw room for growth on this young team, and that was so much like Navy. Instead of being forced to sit on the bench a couple of years as he learned the game, the team would be built around David. That, plus the Spurs' dedication and the city's enthusiasm, helped us decide.

FREDA We had a lot of things to consider. David had so much leverage. He could have said, "I'll go back in the draft and wait." A lot of people might look at San Antonio and say, "Well, the endorsement market is horrible. It's not Chicago or New York or Los Angeles or Atlanta." We were reading in the newspaper all the rhetoric about, "David will never come to San Antonio. San Antonio is getting its hopes up, and he'll never sign with a market that small. He'll probably go to an LA or a Boston or a richer franchise." It was all speculation; I don't know if David was really thinking of signing with anybody else. I know David admired Magic Johnson. When David shared his views on Magic, people concluded he wanted to play with him. Who wouldn't want to play with Magic? I'd want to play with him.

The visit wasn't the final deciding factor. We visited in September and David didn't sign until November. But before we visited the first time, I don't know if David was thinking about signing with anybody. On our way home, we talked on the plane about how nice the people were and how nice the city was, as much as we could see of it in a weekend, and how the team reminded David of the Naval Academy. They were building. They needed a couple of players: a go-to person and someone who could shoot and rebound. David liked the idea of helping rebuild a team. That's exactly what he did at the Naval Academy. San Antonio showed us two important things: (1) the Spurs and the city clearly wanted and needed him and (2) the team had invited us to their city and treated us well. That was a plus.

We went back to Washington, and I remember one day David's attorneys called the house—they directed everything to us—and said the Spurs had called and asked if David had any intention of signing with San Antonio. They wanted to know where they stood. His representatives talked with David, and David decided he would negotiate with the Spurs.

Obviously, the terms had to be right for him to sign. The Spurs knew they had prime rib, and prime rib doesn't come cheap. They paid prime rib price, plus a premium because he had leverage. Because he had so many options, he wasn't pressured into signing just because he needed the bonus or had a lot of college bills.

Chapter Forty-Four
Building a Successful Career

*Help your children learn to balance
their commitments to job, faith, and family.*

David's negotiations were hiccup-quick. His agents asked, and the Spurs gave. The deal made David the richest athlete in history and the richest sailor since Blackbeard. It covered ten years—two in the Navy and eight pro seasons—and was originally valued at $26 million. But it has proven to be worth far more, because if he met certain standards, a clause in the contract dictated he must be paid the average of the NBA's top two deals beginning in his fourth season. Since 1992, his pay has skyrocketed annually.

Of course, most of us can only dream about such salaries and careers. But despite their differences in salaries, David, Kimberly, and Chuck face the same questions we all do: What's the "right" job? What's the "right" place to live? What's the right balance between job and faith and family?

When David retires from basketball in a few years—he won't be one of those players who hangs on until he's forty—he will use his charitable foundation to donate money to organizations that need it and his fame to spread the word of God.

When Kimberly gets her doctorate in a few years, she plans to work with adults in continuing education. But that was not her original plan. "You get into the world and your life changes and you have to use critical and reflective thinking," she says. "I never would have conceived of teaching as a career until I went to grad school. I told one of my advisors, 'I've thought about teaching adults, but what a joke.' He said, 'You ought to think about it. You ought to try it at a community college, and maybe you'll find you do like it.' And that's what I did. My first class was a blessing in disguise. I had the best students, the best class. We had fun. I like where they're going. I like teaching."

When Chuck's military commitment ends in 1998, he'll have to make a similar decision. He likes his job, and he will be a captain by then, but he will also be a licensed minister. Does he give up the military, become a pastor, and get his own church? Does he try to do both the military and the ministry? He wants to get married and have children. How will he juggle all those priorities?

From Day One of his basketball career, this has always been the biggest knock on David: He's so nice, so well-rounded, he hasn't developed that single-minded devotion and nastiness to being the absolute best basketball player he can be. Sometimes he exasperated Paul Evans at Navy, John Thompson in the Olympics, and Larry Brown in his first year in the NBA. David's problem "was that growing up, he didn't know if he wanted to be Mozart, Thomas Edison, or Bon Jovi," Brown said. "He can be in the Hall of Fame. But when I see Patrick Ewing or Hakeem Olajuwon play, I know David isn't there yet. He's got to decide how badly he wants it, how good he wants to be. He's trying, but I don't know if it will ever happen."

David was NBA Rookie of the Year and earned mention as the league's MVP after sparking the Spurs to a thirty-five game improvement, the greatest one-year turnaround in league history—better than the Celtics' thirty-two-game improvement with Larry Bird, better than the Bucks' twenty-nine-game improvement with Kareem Abdul-Jabbar. Coaching great Pat Riley compared David to Bill Russell, "only a better athlete." Center-turned-GM Wayne Embry compared him to Russell, only with "more offense." Center-turned-commentator Jim Chones predicted "he's going to be the best center ever to play the game." Then-Phoenix coach Cotton Fitzsimmons said he surpassed Michael Jordan, Magic Johnson, and Bird as "the greatest impact player the league has seen since Jabbar." Brown called him "the best player of that size I've ever seen."

The Alamo is the country's most famous monument to losing, but David has turned San Antonio into a winner averaging 54 victories a year. Season ticket sales have gone from 2,315 before he was drafted to 12,365, average attendance from 8,010 to 22,449. Without him, the Spurs might have abandoned San Antonio, and taxpayers might have rejected a fifty-three percent tax hike to build the Alamodome.

He has been an All-Star every year and won the award for best overall stats four of six seasons, and yet his talents are so astonishing, his demeanor so serene, his interest so diverse, the critics have always wondered if he couldn't do more. "People have criticized David because he never seems to get upset or show emotion," former Spurs coach John Lucas said. "But what you see is 'The Admiral.' He's always standing at attention." He was even criticized for turning too nice once he became a born-again Christian. "I thought he became a little soft," then-teammate Willie Anderson said last year. "But now he's turned it around. I hear him always talking about being a warrior."

The criticism began to fade when he won his first scoring title in 1994, and Lucas proclaimed, "David is the best basketball player in the game. He's the most talented and the most gifted. Shaquille O'Neal is a great player, but he isn't David. David plays all five positions and does all the things a point guard does. There has never been a player like him anywhere."

And, said Seattle coach George Karl: "I don't think there's any question this is a different David Robinson than we've seen in the past. He's a much more dangerous player. I've always said the man, if he would ever commit to winning, he would be as scary as anybody in the league. I'm not saying he's not committed, but if I saw the face of a lion—an angry warrior type of look—I'd be real nervous."

The warrior won his first MVP trophy last year, but in the playoffs, Olajuwon outplayed him, and the top-seeded Spurs left without rings again. And so the quest for basketball's Olympus continues. Jordan didn't win a title until his seventh year, Olajuwon until his tenth year, Julius Erving until his twelfth year. Patrick Ewing and Charles Barkley still haven't. Like David, Olajuwon played little organized basketball until he got to college, and he's still getting better at age thirty-three. Why shouldn't David, at thirty?

AMBROSE That's the scary part. There's so much he doesn't know. He's been in the league six years and he's still learning. Looking where Hakeem came from versus where David came from—it's very similar. Hakeem was a soccer goalie and hadn't played much basketball. Hakeem has developed quite nicely. So has David. Hakeem has three years on David.

I still don't think David has reached his full potential, because I know what he does and does not do in the offseason. I've talked to him numerous times about it: Instead of doing all the things you do, spend some time on the court and work on new moves. I know he didn't work that hard in the offseason before, but this year he did, perhaps because of maturity or the bitter taste of losing in the semifinals last year.

Once he gains confidence in some new moves, develops some moves people don't know about, he'll be awesome. He has two or three different hooks, but he doesn't use them. He doesn't have the confidence in them because he doesn't work on them enough. He doesn't practice much in the offseason. He starts a month before the preseason. He likes to spend time with his family, and I don't have any problem with that, but if you're going to better yourself, you've got to practice. I used to preach that when they were little: Practice makes perfect. As they got older, perfect practice makes perfect.

I tell him that now and he says, "Okay, Pops." Or "You're right." And then he ignores me. He's a grown man; he can do that. I've done my job. I've let him know what I think. We did that a lot even when they were children. We let them do things on their own and let them see the consequences. I'd say, "This is the way I'd do it. You can do it the way you want and see what works."

DAVID Becoming a Christian has changed my basketball life because it's given me more of a purpose and determination. When I used to play for myself and my own glory, sometimes it was so much harder to be motivated. Because at what point do you have enough money? At what point do you have enough fame? How do you get over the little aches and pains? How do you find the motivation to get up and work out and push yourself harder and harder and harder? Some people have that drive in them. But I never really had that drive. If I could do things well enough for everybody's satisfaction, that was enough. Until people pushed me, I never went past that. But God gave me another reason to excel. He gave me something beyond what anyone on Earth has ever given me. God saw in me a perfection, a place to go I could never envision. It was like letting my Father down if I didn't reach for that. I don't know what my potential is. I don't know what God has in store for me, but if I don't go get it, if I don't push myself toward it, then I have cheated God. There's no way, when I come before him, that I want him to ask me, "What did you do with what I gave you?" and I have to say, "I buried it in the ground."

I have an unbelievable responsibility on the basketball floor to honor what God has given me. It's far more than what I feel toward the fans, and it's far more than what I feel toward the people who pay me or what I feel even toward my teammates. I have a responsibility to come out here and work, make myself better and better, and not for my glory and honor but for his. So that's my drive. God doesn't want wimps. He wants warriors.

God didn't say, "David, we're going to make you lose in the playoffs and we're going to make Hakeem Olajuwon play great so you'll look like a clown." He didn't say that to hurt my feelings. He was trying to say, "David, you need to mature. You need to get stronger. You need to get better. So you can either cry about it or you can get better."

FREDA Should they become workaholics to get ahead? Not by a long shot. The order of their priorities should be: God No. 1, family No. 2, and work No. 3. Without God we'd be nothing. He's the reason for our being. You have to give him the praise for your very being, what you are and what you've accomplished. The family is your nucleus. Nothing can function without a nucleus. The family is your strength, it's your backbone, it's your cover, it's your completeness, it's your support mechanism. You need to work for financial security, but you don't want to forget your priorities.

Chapter Forty-Five
Finding Faith

—————

*It is never too late to discover faith, or
to rediscover religion if you have strayed
from the church.*

Freda has gone to church seemingly forever, but only in
the past dozen years has she become what she considers a true
Christian. Her children abandoned church as soon as they left
for college, but all found themselves unfulfilled until they committed their lives to Christ.

They offer compelling testimony about the path they have
followed to become born again, and what the Lord has meant
to their lives ever since. They recognize faith is a personal
choice, but they share their stories here so that you can consider if you might find the same fulfillment and satisfaction.

FREDA I was a churchgoer all my life, and when you're in a
church, you can always say you're a Christian, but the
word is used loosely much too much. Because you're saying
you're Christ-like and that's a lie if you're not living that life.

I was saved April 11, 1983, after a scare. I had just had my
annual mammogram when my doctor called me at home and
told me he had seen a suspicious area on my X-rays. He thought
he had felt a cyst, but he wanted me to come back that afternoon to be re-examined. After the second exam, he said I

should have a biopsy. He scheduled it for a few days later, and I was petrified. All I could think was, "I have cancer."

When you have a disorder or disease you might die from, it sheds a new light on your life. I thought, "Now I know this can happen to anybody, because it's happening to me. I'm a young woman with children still in school, and I want to finish raising them. I just moved into a new home with a husband I'd like to continue to enjoy." I cried for days.

I realized my faith in God was weak, and I needed prayer. I needed the Lord and I needed to do something about it. As I stood in front of the kitchen window, washing dishes and crying, I asked myself, "Who will pray for me?" My sister Jessie came to mind. She had been saved for years, and she walks, talks, and acts like she is saved. She loves the Lord and has a personal relationship with him. I wanted her to pray for me because I knew the message would get through to the Lord.

I called her, and the minute she heard my voice, she asked, "What's the matter?" I said, "I want you to pray for me. I'm having a biopsy done on my breast," and I told her the date it was scheduled. As I talked, I began to cry. She listened for a moment and said, "You need Jesus." She prayed with me on the phone, and I felt so much better. You see, the prayer of the righteous availeth much.

I reported to the hospital that following Sunday before noon and was admitted to the surgical floor. My surgery was scheduled for Monday morning after I had more mammograms. But that Sunday night as I lay in bed, I began to have aches in my left chest that felt like pleurisy. It was hurting to the point that I couldn't lay on that side. I'd never had any of those symptoms before. The medication nurse gave me my sedatives about 9:30. I even spoke to the patient in the bed next to me about my discomfort. Finally, I fell asleep, and when I woke up the next morning, all the aches and pains were gone. It felt as if I had lost ten pounds, and I wasn't afraid anymore. I knew only the Lord could have done this and it had to have been the prayer of the righteous. He was the only one who could have given me this peace. It was then I said that from this day on, I was giving my life to him. I vowed that when I got up from that bed, I would be a new creature in Christ.

They sent the stretcher at 6:00 A.M. to take me to X-ray to have more film taken. They took film after film. I waited so long in that cold X-ray room, I finally had to ask the technician what was taking so long. She said she didn't know, but soon she returned with my doctor. I asked him the same question, and he sort of shrugged his shoulders and said, "To tell you the truth, the radiologist and I along with a couple of other doctors went over your X-rays, and we don't see the spot anymore. We don't see anything to worry about. I *know* I saw something on the initial X-rays, but we compared them to the ones you just took this morning, and there is nothing on the new X-rays." He then ordered me back to the surgical floor and told me he would be right up to examine me. He started to examine me and said, "I can't believe it. I can't feel anything. " I told him I was ready to have the surgery that day. He said, "No, Freda. We can't cut you if we don't see any reason to." He then discharged me to home, telling me to be in his office in a month.

My husband took me home and I slept off the anesthesia. When I woke up, I called my sister to let her know the results and began to tell her I was okay and the doctors didn't find anything. I told her about the aches and pains in my left side that I'd had the Sunday night before surgery. She asked me what time that had been, and I told her it was around 9 P.M. She said she knew I was all right. She then said that Sunday evening she had been in church praying at the altar, and she sensed something being destroyed in her chest. The Lord revealed to her he had healed the tumor in my chest.

I saw the doctor a month later, and everything was fine. From that day on, it was history.

One day I was speaking to a lady who was afraid because her doctor had found a lump in her breast. I told her what God had done for me, and I told her to have faith, but she just laughed at me as if I were a silly woman. I know she didn't believe, but I know what God has done for me. I know it was not coincidence. I know God is real, and he will take care of us.

I know he has the power. It makes you see yourself for what you are. It makes you feel not so alone anymore. We tend to think we have a lot of time and that we're the ones in control. But life is short and we're not in control. When things happen, I don't think they're coincidences. I think there's a reason for everything that happens and a season for everything.

Since then, I've gotten my life in order. I have served the Lord faithfully. I love the Lord. I treat him like I love him. I'm not trying to be fanatical. I'm just grateful that the Lord has allowed me the things he has. I'm grateful to be alive.

As they were growing up, I told all of my children about the Lord, but I could not make them drink. They received him when they were ready.

DAVID As children, we went to church because Mom said we had to. I had a kind of faith, but it was never an important issue for me. It was just there. Did it matter in my life? Not really. I knew the stories about Jesus, but they were just like fairy tales. To a lot of kids, they're just neat stories, the same kind of stories you read in the history books about George Washington or different battles. Do they matter or affect what you do today or tomorrow? No. That's the attitude I had for the longest time. Faith was never a big part of my life until I was born again in 1991.

When I went to the Naval Academy and didn't *have* to go to church, I stopped going. I'd go on occasion, but I can count on one hand the number of times. I don't think we were resentful Mom made us go, but it wasn't exciting for us.

I wouldn't say I was unhappy, but my life was unsatisfying. And it was peculiar it was unsatisfying because I had so much. Chuck would come to visit me and he'd love it. Everyone would look at me and say, "Boy, you've got it made. Man, alive, you should really be enjoying this. It's awesome." And I wasn't. It was nice, but it wasn't satisfying, it wasn't fulfilling.

I had a lot, but I started wondering, "Here I am with five cars, two houses, and more money than I ever thought I'd have. What more could I ask for? But where am I going?" Here's

Michael Jordan, he has more than me, and boy, I'd like to have some of the things he has, but is the world setting a trap for us? We win the NBA championship trophy, but is winning one trophy enough? Is winning five trophies enough? There's always something else. Twenty years from now, who will really care? Bill Russell has won eleven championships. That's really great, it really is. That's an unbelievable accomplishment. But one day it will all be over. The things Bill Russell has accomplished mean far less than who he is as a person and how he affects people's lives.

I realized all I was pursuing couldn't fulfill me. I was a successful athlete making a lot of money, but if I couldn't be happy with myself, something was wrong. Ninety-nine percent of the people in the world would want to be in my shoes, but I was still looking for more. That's what shocked me into waking up. What I had should have been plenty, but no matter how much I had, it didn't seem like enough because material things can't satisfy our deepest needs. That's when I started to realize I needed the Lord.

Back in 1986 at the World Championships, I'd had the same unsettling feeling. On the way back from Amsterdam, an evangelist on the plane talked to us about Christ. I prayed with him, but I didn't understand what I was doing. It sounded good, but I really didn't get it. For the next five years, I knew there had to be more to this Christianity stuff. I called myself a Christian because I had prayed with that evangelist, but Christ hadn't become real to me. In the back of my mind, I knew there had to be more.

Everyone has his own moment when he comes face to face with God. For me there was one dramatic episode. On June 8, 1991, a minister came from Austin to San Antonio. He was there with a group called Champions for Christ. He and I talked, and he asked me some questions. The first question he asked was, "David, do you love God?" I was a little surprised and said, "Of course I love God." Then he asked, "How much time do you spend praying?" I said, "Every once in a while. I eat three times a day, and I pray then." Then he asked me, "How much time do you spend reading your Bible?" I answered, "There's one around here somewhere. I've got one. I just don't understand it. It doesn't make a lot of sense to me." He said, "When you love someone, don't you usually take time to get to know that person? Don't you want to know that certain person better?"

To be honest, when he said that, the first thing I thought was, "God is not a real person." But that day, Christ became a real person to me. The minister asked me one more question: "The Old Testament says to set aside one day a week to honor God. When was the last time you spent one day, not one day a week, just one day, to praise God and thank him for what you have?" I realized I had never done that. I felt like a spoiled brat. Everything was about me, me, me. How much money can I make? It was all about David's praise and David's glory. Everybody cheering David. Everybody patting David on the back. I had never stopped to honor God for all he had done for me. That really hit me and I just cried. I cried all afternoon, and I prayed and told the Lord, "Everything you've given me, I'm giving back to you today." That was a big moment in my life.

It was obvious the Lord had sent him because it was the first time I was really affected by what someone said about God. I started to think, "Where am I going? What am I doing? Who am I as a man? What makes me any different than the next guy?" In all honesty, I knew nothing really made me different than the next guy. The Lord showed me that without him, I had nothing. That was a scary thought. All the money, everything I had—without him, I had nothing.

That very day, I was saved. I committed myself to him that day.

As I committed myself to the Lord, he began to bless me in a great way. He opened up all my senses and I began to put my energy into reading and studying the Bible. I was pretty spread out at that time. I was into everything: music, basketball, playing golf, and doing all kinds of different things. But I just dropped everything and got into the Word and into fellowship with other believers. During the next two months, God blessed me with a lot of knowledge and a ton of wisdom. Because it was summer, it was easy to immerse myself in the Word and sur-round myself with Christian friends who could build me up spiritually. But when the season started again—and I was around a lot of guys with lifestyles and values that were differ-ent from mine—I really had to be strong. And so, since that summer, I've been on fire. My goal is to get my teammates and friends to understand that God is tapping them on the shoulder and telling them it's time to get right with him.

No question, faith has drawn me closer to my family, because other people in my family have gotten saved, too. Chuck and I have always been close, but when I first got saved we weren't as close because we didn't have things in common to talk about. I wanted to talk about the Lord; he wanted to talk about girls. We didn't talk as much, and as deeply, but when he gave his life to the Lord, we became closer than ever. It's the same way with my sister and my mother. We have a much deeper understanding of each other because of our relationship with the Lord.

It was also the turning point in my relationship with Valerie. We were broken up at the time I got saved. We weren't even communicating with one another. I never thought about getting back together with Valerie until the Lord put it in my heart. When I first got saved, I told the Lord, "Please don't put any women in my life." I didn't want to date anybody. Before I could learn to be committed to a woman, I knew I had to learn to be committed to him. Following that, a commitment to a girl-friend and then my wife would be easy. Valerie and I were apart about nine months when the Lord led me back to her. He put in my heart, showed me, "This is the girl I've placed in your life. Your relationship before was without me, and it's typical for a worldly relationship to deteriorate like that, but with me, it'll be a whole new relationship." And it has been.

She was doing her own searching while we were apart and had gotten saved just after I did. The Lord had started working in her heart, too. She started thinking about me again.

Some couples work out a prenuptial agreement before they get married to give them some sort of peace. But God says if a man honors his wife and nourishes and cherishes her, the two of them will be one. That's where my fulfillment comes from.

I get fulfillment out of pleasing God, knowing I'm doing the things he's calling me to do. My satisfaction comes in knowing God is smiling down on me as a husband and father. When he sees my effort on the basketball floor, he knows I'm doing it for his glory. And he's pleased with that.

As long as he's in control, I'm in good shape. I don't have to know what's coming. That's a great feeling: not having to worry about the future. I mean, for example, one of the biggest worries a parent has is, "How will my kids turn out? Will they be an embarrassment to me? Will they be prosperous? Will they be equipped to handle the world?" I don't have to worry about that. It's one of the big pluses. I know they may go astray for a while, but as long as we give them the basics, as long as we show them who God is and instill in them that love and that passion for him, God gives me the peace to know they'll come back. I love them. I spend my time with them. As a father, I honor them, and I know God smiles on me because I do that. So I have a peace and a satisfaction that I can't get anywhere else.

Serving the Lord is the central point of everything I do. Like I get up this morning and go change my son's diaper and try to make life for my wife easier and better, not because I feel guilty, but because I want to honor her today. I want to nourish her and see her grow. That's a commitment I feel as much to God as to her. God has given me a beautiful wife and two incredible kids. I couldn't have made these kids on my own. They're just incredible little creations. So he's the central point of my existence, just like a human father is to his child.

Christianity is a powerful lifestyle choice. The most powerful man ever was Jesus. He never backed down from anybody, and I believe that's how he wants us to live. We've got to get into people's lives and challenge them with God's truth. Some things aren't negotiable in this world, and one of them is God's standards. He never said they were easy to follow, but when you know him, you know they're right.

Most athletes are in sports for the competition. The joy is in the competition against an enemy, an opponent. You want to win at all costs. Now, if we compare that to life, the devil is our biggest enemy, our biggest opponent. Not only is he very capable, but on his terms, we're sure to lose the competition.

If you walk with God, you can have victory, even when things get really tough. So the challenge is to walk with God. Sounds pretty simple, but therein lies the battle. For example, how many people get married and say to each other, "I love you, we'll be together for the rest of our lives," and end up not being together for the rest of their lives? What makes a person, four or five years after getting married, look at the other person and say, "I don't love you anymore"? What happens is, the devil gets in there and plays his tricks and separates the couple and builds wedges between them, and they end up losing the battle. Something that was very special, probably the most special thing in their lives, they end up losing. Well, God says we don't have to lose the battle. It is something he gives us for the rest of our lives.

People break promises to each other all the time. When someone says, "I guarantee you I won't do this," that's worth about as much as it weighs. I don't care how good you feel about that person's trustworthiness, the person may let you down sometime. But God will never let us down. The reason my wife and I would never even consider divorce is not because we're so much better than everybody else and have no problems, but because we made a vow to God. We want to keep it because God always keeps his vows to us.

CHUCK As children, we went to church because that was one of the rules of the house. Like a chore; if you were supposed to clean your room before you went to bed, that was what you did. Every Sunday, we knew we were supposed to go to church, and so we didn't question, didn't argue. Well, sometimes we did, but church was just something we had to do. It's not something we necessarily desired to do, but just going and being in that environment certainly had an effect on us. Little kids pick up things. Whether we thought we were paying attention or not, we picked up things. We learned about Jesus, we learned about what God likes and doesn't like and, regardless of whether we were living it or not at the time, it stayed with us.

Just like David, once I went to college and I didn't have to go to church anymore, I didn't go unless it was Easter or Thanksgiving or Christmas. Before I graduated, I put my orders in for three bases in Virginia and Maryland and three in San Antonio. I figured I couldn't go wrong. The Air Force had six bases where different members of my family lived. I knew I was set. And then when I graduated, I got my orders and they said Biloxi, Mississippi. I went to the recruiter, a captain in the Air Force, and said, "Sir, there must be a mistake here." He looked at me and said, "Welcome to the military."

I didn't know that was the Lord working in my life. Biloxi was the last place on earth I would have ever thought about. The only thing I knew about Biloxi was the movie Biloxi Blues, and I didn't like that movie. The only other thing I knew about Mississippi was the movie Mississippi Burning, and I didn't like that movie, either. Well, I got to Biloxi and I'm from the East Coast, the Washington D.C. area, and I'm used to a real up-to-date, fast-paced life. But people in Biloxi then were still wearing clothes we wore two years before. They still wore hairstyles we had four years before. They talked slower. Everything was slower. Everything was so country. I hated it those first three or four months.

My brother had been saved for two years and had preached to me for two years. I would hate to come home because, man, he would just wear me out. We would be up until 3 in the morning and he'd be sitting there showing me stuff in the Bible. "Look at this! This is great stuff! Can you believe it?" And I'd be sitting there, saying, "I've got a date. I've got to get going." I was living that bachelor lifestyle and I was loving it. I got so sick of David preaching to me, I started to stay at my mom's house when I came home, and sometimes I'd try to avoid him.

It sunk in, though, because I saw how happy he was and how much peace he had. That's what the Lord does for you. He gives you this peace to where you could wreck your new car and of course you'd have to deal with it, but you'd still have peace. I saw how happy David was, how good his marriage was, how happy my mother was after she got saved, and I wanted that.

I was driving home on New Year's Eve from New Orleans, and it was just like a cartoon show where Bugs Bunny is faced with the decision to do good or bad.

A little devil on one shoulder is saying, "Do bad things. Do bad things."

A little angel with a halo is on the other shoulder saying, "Do the right thing. Do the right thing."

And it was just like that on that hour-and-fifteen-minute-drive home. One voice would tell me, "Man, I want to be like my brother and I want to be like my mother and I want to be happy and not worry about things and not be sad all the time and have this empty space in my life."

And then the other voice would tell me, "Well, you can't date her and you can't date her and you can't date her and you can't date her."

And the other voice would say, "And you'll get to go to heaven."

And the other voice would say, "You can't date her!"

And the other voice would say, "You'll have joy."

And the other voice would say, "You can't date her any-more."

Finally, I heard the Lord say, "Look, just make up your mind. Either you're going to be happy or you're not. If you're not going to be happy, you should stop debating whether you want to be saved or not. If you just want to go ahead and keep sinning, go ahead and do it and don't feel remorse about it."

And so, during that drive, I made up my mind. I said, "I'm going to give my life to the Lord. I can't lose. If I try it and I don't like it, I can always go back. I can't go wrong."

I had met some people in Biloxi who invited me to church, and I ended up giving my life to the Lord the next day. That was at the beginning of 1994.

I didn't expect to ever like Mississippi. But I got to the place where I didn't want to leave it, didn't want to leave my church. Had I not gotten saved two years ago, I know I'd be real unhappy about now. I'd try to date everybody, and you never know, I might have had AIDS by now. I have a tendency to fall asleep driving; I might have wrecked my car and be dead now. I didn't drink—I didn't like the taste of alcohol—but I did the normal bad stuff. I was what people would call a good, moral person, but I knew that wouldn't get me into heaven.

We're all born with this void in our spirit. We try to fill it with different things; a new car, a great house, a wife, children. But the only thing that can fill that void is the Lord. When Jesus comes in, it's just amazing. It's been less than two years and I want to preach and I want to teach and I want to do all this stuff.

I have a brother who's saved and a mother who's saved and a sister who's saved . . . like David said, our relationship is on a totally different level now. We've always been close friends, but now we have so much more to talk about, so much more in common. We're six years and eight inches apart, but people always ask me, "Are you two twins?" We do look a lot alike, but now, we're alike in our way of thinking. Man, I couldn't ask for anything better to happen to my family and to me.

KIMBERLY My mother was the reason we went to church. When we moved to Green Run in Virginia Beach in 1973, we started going to Trinity Church. I was in about fourth grade, when you begin to comprehend things, and just really got involved in the church. They had all these youth groups, almost like a Girl Scout group, and I really liked it. Sometimes I wanted to go more than my parents wanted to take us. If my mom had to work on Sunday, we'd ask my dad. He might say, "Nah." And we'd say, "Can you take us then?" and he'd drop us off. But Mom would go with us.

After we left Virginia Beach and I got to be of driving age, I had other interests and lost some interest in the church. I'd think, "This is okay for kids, but I've outgrown it." I'd go just to keep the peace because my mom would say you couldn't do anything else the rest of the day if you didn't go to church in the morning. In college it wasn't important to me. I was away from home. I had friends who were saved, and I thought they were taking it too far. My mother would ask me if I'd gone to church and I'd say, "I saw it on TV." I thought that was enough. We had a chapel on campus for noonday prayer. I went a couple of times and thought, "Yeah, this is pretty nice."

After I got out of college and started working, I'd go to church out of habit, but I didn't feel I was getting anything out of it. One day I was sitting in some church and the minister asked, "Will there be one?" and I started thinking about being saved. I knew I needed to find my own church, my own place. And so I started actively seeking out churches that I could call home. A church should be family.

Finally, I found a church that I wanted to join, and that was a day to remember. The minister asked, "Anyone like to give your life to the Lord?" and I went up to the altar. Then I went back into a little vestibule where the church secretary asked me my name, but I couldn't speak. It was so weird, like someone had knocked the wind out of me, like a supernatural force was trying to keep me from giving the information. I felt dizzy and almost lost my balance. When I told one of my friends about it later, she joked, "That was the devil trying to get one last shot at you." But that made me think. It probably *was* the devil trying to get one last shot.

The day I got baptized—February 18, 1993—a lot of things came to a head for me. I went to work that day and my baptism was that night. All day, all I could think about was getting baptized. Baptists are not sprinkled like Catholics are, but are submerged in water. It was winter and I was thinking, "It will be freezing. Sparks will fly out of the water." But when I got up there, it was like the water was tempered just for me. I didn't want to get out. I had the feeling of closure, like I was getting rid of the dead and starting anew, doing away with old ways. The old Kim was dead. Now there was a new me. My mother was always spiritual. I had lost my way, but that day I found it again.

I have made that church my home. I come out of each service a different person, because I've been spiritually fed. I write for the church newspaper and attend Bible study and Saturday Bible class. I've become proactive in my own spiritual growth.

My way of thinking has really changed. For example, before, if I had gone to the grocery store and received ten dollars too much in change, I would have kept it. Now I would give it back. It's just a lot of little things like that. Being polite. Being courteous. Big things started to happen when I changed little things in my life. Before, I always said I got my MBA because I had self-confidence. Now, I feel if I have any confidence, it's because the Lord gave it to me. I used to believe in luck. Not anymore. I believe in blessings. Don't wish me luck. Wish me blessings.

Chapter Forty-Six
Money Can't Buy Me Love

Do not pursue money, success, and fame with a blind passion, for they do have their down sides, and they will fail to bring you true happiness.

The Robinsons—not just David but to an extent the whole family—have learned not only the perks but the price of fame. They have met the past four presidents. They have made all-expenses-paid trips to swank resorts to play as celebrities in pro-am golf tournaments. They sat in the Ripken family box the night Cal Ripken Jr. broke Lou Gehrig's record for consecutive games played. They have hobnobbed with celebrities in and out of sports. David has jammed on the saxophone with two of his jazz heroes, Grover Washington and Branford Marsalis.

They can go anywhere in San Antonio, and not just David but Ambrose and Freda, too, are addressed with a reverence befitting royalty. Ambrose is addressed as "Mr. Robinson," Freda is showered with honors and awards, and one local executive even flies them to Houston on his private jet just to dine with them.

Chuck and Kim come to visit and people want to know them because they have a famous brother, a mixed blessing. People assume that because David is a millionaire that no one else works for a living, and while it is true he has given them beautiful gifts—

an expensive car or a computer or college funds—he does not (and they do not want him to) support them.

Privacy is nil. When David had a bad stomach flu once after office hours and went to the emergency room, the "news" made newspapers nationwide and top-of-the-page headlines in the San Antonio newspaper. The local ABC affiliate broke into the start of Monday Night Football to breathlessly give a special report.

Three separate guards or gates must be passed to get to David's house, and still, fans have hopped the fence and gotten to the door. Innocent? Maybe, but the way the world is today, how can you tell the difference between an overexuberant fan and a demented criminal? David cannot go anywhere without being swarmed for his autograph, but he tries not to let it bother him anymore, and adds a scripture verse beneath his signature in hopes the autograph seeker seeks out God, too. You say he has an obligation because he's an athlete? Maybe, but how would you like to be followed and watched every hour of every day? Would you be in a good mood and act perfectly twenty-four hours a day with everyone pulling on you, with every word you say open to public second-guessing?

David's fame forces Chuck and Kim to examine would-be friends with a suspicious eye. David's money forces him to evaluate what is important in life. He is not a spendthrift. Still, David once said his wealth challenged him spiritually, and he struggled to draw the line between possessing things and things possessing him. His biggest fear was he wouldn't be a good person and go to heaven because "the Bible says it's harder for a rich man to find his way into the Kingdom of Heaven than it is for a camel to pass through the eye of a needle."

DAVID Before I got saved, I couldn't understand that scripture for anything. But when the Lord started to open up my heart, I began to understand that being rich in his eyes and being rich in a worldly way are a whole lot different. You're in a lot of trouble if you're rich in a worldly way but you're not rich in his eyes. He's saying you can't carry a lot of extra baggage into heaven. The passage isn't big enough. So if you're going to come to him, you've got to come with a pure heart and with no other agenda. I know I don't have any other agenda in life. My agenda is to please God and do his will.

FREDA I never knew he worried about that, but I often read that passage and hoped he had read it and gotten the true meaning out of it. Because so often, society makes rich people feel guilty. You've got to know yourself, you've got to be yourself, and you've got to have the right priorities. If you don't have the right priorities, you can have all the money and all the education in the world and still be a fool.

Money is something he's prayed about, asking the Lord to keep his mind set correctly as to how to use it. When people have money, others prey on them, and I can see why some fall into drugs or promiscuity. Money and status don't cause them to fall; it's their misuse of their finances.

There's nothing wrong with money. What's wrong is to love money so much that it becomes the sole purpose of your life. Your life should be worth more than that. Living is more important. Money can be an asset, but the love of it and the need for it can destroy you. Money is not everything. Some people have more money than they can ever spend in a lifetime, but they're not happy. If you're happy, that's what counts.

You shouldn't teach children, "You have to have status, you have to have money." I never want my children to be class-conscious. I don't care what a person has. You can have class without having money.

I look at myself as a regular person, but others don't. They see me as David Robinson's mother. They don't see Freda Robinson, who had three children and for thirty-some years worked hard for a living, working all shifts for low pay. I'd like to have my own identity. They think I've never known what it's like to go without, but I have. They look at me as if I were a millionaire, but I'm not. I'm a poor-naire.

A lady at church was having a problem with finances and told me, "Oh, well, you wouldn't know about living from day to day." I said, "Yes I would. I've been on both sides of the fence."

I also hear this: "Oh, your son will buy it for you." I remember talking to someone about some expensive clothing and saying, "I can't afford that; that's out of my league." And she said, "Ask your son!" I said, "My son has a family to support." I shouldn't be running to him, begging for this and that. He's nice enough to me. It's not like he's never done anything for us. I've got my own husband, and we should live in our own league. You tell people that and it runs off them like water over grease.

KIMBERLY A lot of people think trickle-down economics are in effect. They think I'm crazy to work all these jobs. They ask, "What are you doing that for? Why don't you ask your brother for a car? I can't believe you drive this car." I remember when I was working at Safeway to help pay for college—one of the best things that ever happened because I learned I wanted more out of life than that—and people thought David was making us live a pitiful life.

We can't just ride on his coattails. No. 1, it's not me. No. 2, even if I wanted a free ride, I don't know that he'd let me. I think he'd want me to make more out of my life.

But David would do anything to help with our education. When he found out I was going back to school to get my master's, he called and said, "If you want help while you're going back to school, let me know. I'll support you if you want to do anything to better yourself. Don't sweat it. Don't run around and go crazy." I was working full time and going to school full time. I was struggling. Yes, I took enough money to pay for college; I'm not an idiot. He wanted me to quit my full-time job so I could concentrate on school, and I wouldn't do that. I figured you're more marketable if you have your degree *and* a job. I couldn't justify quitting my job. I was getting prime experience in my field. And I needed to make my own money. I'm used to working. That's the bottom line.

CHUCK People have the misconception that David gave me everything, and very few really know the truth. And that's fine. The world will think a certain way and you can't control that, but I don't feel it's necessary to tell people, "Well, I paid for my Lexus." I don't need to show them my auto title and pay stub. People will come up and say, "Are you David's brother?" And I'll say yes and they'll say, "Let me see your ID." I'll look at them like, "That's not necessary. If you don't believe what I tell you, that's fine." My life doesn't depend on whether or not someone believes I am who I say I am.

People identify me because of David, but I have my own identity. I fought hard to keep out of my circle people who just wanted to know me because of my brother. People saying, "Are you David Robinson's little brother? How's your brother doing?" That happens to me more often than I stop at a stop sign. It's just like stopping at a stop sign in that it's something I have to do. I couldn't pull up all the stop signs in the world. It's just the way life is, the way people are.

At one time, I'm sure it frustrated me and I didn't handle it as well as I do now. That's another reason why I've never allowed many people to get close to me, because most people approach me that way. They feel comfortable coming to me because they know who my brother is, and so immediately a wall forms. I'll be nice to them, but that might be the last time I talk to them. Too often, they don't want to know me. They just want to know about him. So that conversation lasts five seconds.

FREDA It's not easy on the other siblings when one is put on a pedestal. It pressures the other kids to the point where they need to rise some more. David's fame has to affect them, which is why it's so important for the other children to be well-rounded, so it doesn't bother them as much. They can't compete with his fame and money, but they all got their degrees—and Kim's working on her third. And Chuck has done great. Here's a kid who was a good student in high school and went on to graduate from the Naval Academy and is studying for the ministry. There's not much more they could do.

But they're almost like forgotten children. When you take people's identity away from them, that's negative. We shouldn't live in the shadow of anyone else. When reporters would interview Chuck and call him "David's little brother," Chuck would get bent out of shape. He would tell them, "I'm my own person. I'm not David's little brother. I'm Chuck Robinson." He was really adamant. I can understand why he wanted to be Chuck and not David's little brother. All of us need our own identity. Kim was more reserved and didn't talk about it as much, but it had to bother her. One time she told me, "They never mention me," and a lot of times, reporters told me, "We didn't know he had a sister." That's the down side.

Chuck played basketball at Navy, but he played in the shadow of David. David broke thirty-three records up there. So the expectations were so much greater for Chuck, even though the Navy officials say, "We're not going to brand you or expect you to do the same thing as David." He wasn't ridiculed, but he wasn't always a happy camper up there.

CHUCK I came to college 6'3", 185, and left at 6'5", 195. I felt my whole time at Navy, the expectations for me were higher than for everybody else. That wasn't unusual for me because my parents had expected a lot, too, but it's still not right for the coaches to do that. Whether they did it purposely or subliminally, I knew it was there. The coaches would yell at me more, get on me more. They'd play me according to whether they thought I was reaching the potential they thought I had. It was real frustrating at times. Everybody—sports fanatics, players on other teams—would say, "What's wrong with your coach? You don't play very much." Sometimes I'd be playing a whole bunch and sometimes I wouldn't. I'd start the season averaging thirty-eight minutes a game and end the season averaging two minutes.

When I picked the same college David went to, I knew what I'd be facing because I faced it all through high school. It just increased in college. I could have gone somewhere else. I had basketball scholarships to other schools, and I could have played ball for them. But I could not allow what other people think to affect my life decisions. And going to the Naval Academy was a life decision. I said, "If I decide not to go to the Naval Academy and I wind up a bum and a beggar at forty-five, I'll kick myself and say, 'I could have gone to the Naval Academy.'" My mom will tell you, I've never allowed outsiders to change my decisions.

My parents had always set high standards for David, and he had always met them and could just do everything real well, and so I was expected to do that, too. My parents never said, "Your brother can do this and that," but I knew how high they esteemed him. Everyone saw him in a real high light because of his intelligence, his athletic ability. He was gifted, one of the smartest people I've ever known. He has the book knowledge, he can do everything, and he's interested in everything. He's always amazed me.

I fought hard for my own identity, but there were plenty of pluses. When I was in high school, other kids would say, "We rode our BMXs all weekend" and I'd say, "Well, I just got back from the White House with my brother." How many sixteen-year-olds get to ride in limos and meet Dr. J and hang out with Magic Johnson and go to the Mike Tyson fight with M.C. Hammer? I wasn't accustomed to, but I was exposed to, a little more lavish lifestyle, so eventually, meeting Michael Jordan was no longer a big thing to me and seeing people drive a Mercedes wasn't a big thing to me, even though we didn't have one. I was exposed to that lifestyle, so that's why now, the Lord can do some things for me and it won't take me away from him. Cars break and houses burn, but the Lord will always be there.

KIMBERLY I haven't lived in David's shadow. When David became well known, I was already grown. I'd have to honestly say all of this has been more positive than negative. The question people always ask me is, "What's it like to have a famous brother?" My response is, "Do you have a brother or sister? We get along the same way." A lot of people think fame and fortune changes people. David has more resources to do what he wants, but if anything has changed, he's gotten a bigger heart.

Even if you stripped away basketball and notoriety, David still has more going for him as a person than the average guy, more than anyone could want. He has a big heart, he's generous, he's kind, he loves teaching people. It warms me to see what he's done for other people, and I don't mean just family, but even strangers. He can do things other people only dream about. He doesn't have to be the sole beneficiary of his success. Not just monetarily, either. He has insights and wisdom to share. He can speak on any topic on a dime. You can catch him anywhere and ask him a question and he can give you an intelligent answer.

Being his sister has many positives. I don't see the negatives. I was eight years older than Chuck, so I have a different vantage point. Most of my friends knew me long before David became "The Admiral." When David got famous, Chuck was at an age where kids admired pro athletes and would want to hang around Chuck because of his brother. I was at a different stage of my life. When I went out on dates, I never brought up David's name. I saw how other brothers and sisters of famous athletes acted—as if they were the ones who were famous and making all the money. I remember one girl at Howard who really thought she was something special because her brother played basketball. I didn't want to act like that.

The black population in San Antonio is very minute. I don't go there as often as Chuck does, but when I do, they want to get to know me. Many of them do seem to have ulterior motives—to know David through me. I guarantee that the people I've met in my age group, I don't think they've been interested in knowing me for me. But it doesn't bother me. I'm in Virginia, getting on with my life. I have no desire to try to keep up with David. There's no sibling rivalry. No way. Trust me. We're all different hues. There's no way I'd try to compete.

Chapter Forty-Seven
Giving Something Back

━━━━━━━━━━

Give a little piece of your heart, and the world will be a better place. Share your blessings.

David Robinson stared at the camera and bared a Doberman disposition.

"Mr. Robinson doesn't like garbage in his shoes," he said and snarled. "If you're into drugs, don't come into my neighborhood. Mr. Robinson doesn't like garbage in his neighborhood."

He was selling shoes. But he was also selling an attitude. The Mr. Robinson's Neighborhood commercials—takeoffs on PBS' *Mr. Rogers' Neighborhood*—always offered lessons for youngsters.

Another commercial featured his mother and Georgetown coach John Thompson.

"It's Coach Thompson and my mom with today's word. What's *stupid*?" David asked viewers.

"Not listening to coach Thompson is stupid.

"Not listening to your mom is stupid.

"Dropping out of school is stupid.

"And," he concluded, his face practically jumping into yours, "always listen to your mom."

This wasn't just some sales pitch and phony acting job. This was the essence of David Robinson.

One child drops out of school every ten seconds, and David Robinson wants to do something about it. Too many children can't afford college, or get hooked on drugs, or get pregnant, and David Robinson wants to do something about all that.

We hear a lot today about selfish athletes and egotistical millionaires, but David has strong interests in building better communities, churches, and children. And his involvement doesn't end when the red light goes off.

Even before he became a born-again Christian, he wanted to give something back to the community. Since being saved, he has tithed ten percent of his earnings, and because David's earnings are so significant, in December 1992 he formed The David Robinson Foundation so he can spread his generosity not just to his church but to many charities, as well. In its first four years, it donated more than one million dollars to scores of organizations, and endowed another million dollars to ensure the foundation continues into the next generation of Robinsons.

"The donations typically go to children's charities, especially those that emphasize moral and spiritual guidance. David definitely prefers those with a religious bent, but he funds a wide variety," says Mary Havel, executive director of The David Robinson Foundation. "Some of the charities provide children with jackets and shoes for the cold weather. Some are after-school programs. Some are youth camps with spiritual components. Some stress abstinence. He's sending five kids to a camp in Aspen and twenty at-risk kids to Branson, Missouri. He bought a van for Boys Town so they could get the boys to the church services of their choice. Every Christmas, we have a Christmas Toy Drive, where fans bring toys to the arena, to this office, to corporate sponsors. We've gotten 3000, 4000, 5000 toys a year. David usually hits two or three charities himself to give away some of the toys. We have a celebrity golf tournament every year. The first two years, it earned over $100,000, and it reached $150,000 in '95. Other than what the golf tournament earns, all of our donations are David's money. Occasionally, someone will send in a $25 gift, but David doesn't want a lot of corporate sponsors, doesn't want his to just be seed money."

David doesn't donate just his money and name. He donates time and passion, too. He tapes scads of public-service announcements endorsing the Navy and abstinence and decrying drugs. Number fifty donates fifty tickets to every Spurs home game to children who've been nominated by their teachers for oustanding achievement.

And in 1991, he sponsored the entire fifth-grade class at Gates Elementary School in the national "I Have A Dream Foundation." He committed to providing $2,000 scholarships to each of the ninety-two children if they go on to graduate from high school and qualify to attend college. He told them he gained nothing from the pledge—indeed, he "could buy a nice Porsche with this money"—but warned them to take their education seriously so they can make something of themselves.

They are ninth-graders now, scattered throughout twenty different high schools, and David attends about half of their monthly gatherings, which includes annual cookouts at his parents' home. Eighty-five percent are black, one hundred percent are minorities, and ninety percent qualify for the school lunch program. Once they graduate, David will open up his scholarship program to competition from all around the city. "As competitive as he is, David doesn't want to just hand scholarships to anyone who graduates," says Havel.

The TV show *60 Minutes*, that beacon of hard-hitting investigative journalism, tracked David for a full week, and this is what announcer Ed Bradley said he uncovered: "This is one hero with a passion for kids and a sense of obligation." Bradley told how David, while still in college, had become a big brother to an Annapolis high school student, Clifford Johnson, and now was paying for his college education.

"This kid could have gone either way," David told Ed Bradley. "I invested my time and love and hopefully made a difference. Now his life is headed in the right direction, and I don't care what happens, I won't let him fall. If he needs a job, I'll take care of him."

"Why are kids so important to you?" Bradley asked.

"If you make a kid believe he can do anything, then he can," David replied. "I don't care where he grows up. They have it all in their hands. It's up to us to guide them, to show them where to go."

And that's what David does, through his donations and frequent talks to children in schools, churches, and homes for the disadvantaged.

"I have the greatest job in the world, playing basketball," he told one group of children. "But there are also a lot of pressures, a lot of stresses. What do I face pressures with? Drugs? People know I have a lot of money, so they come to me and say, 'You wanna buy these drugs?' And I say, 'Nooooo, thank you. I don't want those things. Those things will mess me up for life. I won't be able to do the things I can do on the court.' And you guys won't be able to do the things you want to with your life if you get caught up in drugs. I've seen a lot of guys who've had so many problems with drugs, and it hurts them so badly. It takes away a lot of your dreams, it really does. You can always recover from a mistake, but sometimes you can't repair the damage you do with drugs."

"David's fulfillment in life has really come through how he touches other people's lives," says cousin Aldrich Mitchell, the senior vice president of The Robinson Group. "David believes true satisfaction in life is achieved when you are concerned not only for yourself but for others, as well. David is one of those rare superstars who doesn't just revel in his fame and fortune, but uses it as a means to better other people's lives."

Monsignor Marvin Duerfler of St. Peter's & St. Joseph's Children's Home says the message is getting through: "There's a saying that you never stand so tall as when you stoop to hold a child—and that's what David is doing. He and Valerie are reaching down and pulling up these kids to give them a chance."

Havel, who spent three and a half years as the Spurs' community relations coordinator before leading the charitable foundation, says Sean Elliott is the only Spurs player whose community involvement comes "remotely close to David's." She

216

sometimes speaks as often as eight times a week with David, and even more often with Valerie, the foundation's president.

"David wants to give glory to God through what he does with his foundation," Havel says. "He gets paid well and wants to enrich other people's lives, too. He's definitely every bit of what his public persona is. People ask me, 'What's he really like? He's not as good as they say he is, is he?' Well, he's even better than, even holier than who he seems to be. You scratch the surface of most stars, and the veneer is thin. With David, it goes deep. The wisdom he brings is older than his years."

DAVID The foundation grew out of my wife's and my desire to put something back into the community. We have been so overwhelmingly blessed, we just try to make ourselves tools for God to use. The more he blesses us, the more we'll put back into the program. We want to touch as many people and reach as many lives as we can. We feel really good about what God's doing. Sometimes we get caught up in our own little world and we forget God is so large and he's moving in so many places. He's going to bring us all together one day.

We're still not even making a dent in what San Antonio needs as a city. But maybe somebody else will start to do more because of what we've done. And if you get a lot of people working together, you start making a big difference.

Giving something back has always been a big part of my life. But no matter how much you give back, it means absolutely *nothing* if it's for the wrong reasons. In 1 Corinthians 13, God says, What good is it if you give all you have to the poor but you don't have love in your heart? You gain nothing. That's something that should stick with everybody. You can have a foundation. You can do all kinds of nice things for people. But if you don't have love in your heart, if you're not serving God, it means nothing. You gain nothing from it. That's an unsettling thought. So it's not just the money we donate. It's honoring the Lord with the first fruits of my labor.

FREDA When you have a lot of money, you have what some people call clout—I call it influence—and it can make a big difference. Much is required of whom much is given. That's no more than right. A Scripture in the Bible speaks to that. This is why, when I see people who can afford to help someone else but do not, I feel something is wrong. I tithe in church and a lot of times, I say, "Could I have afforded more this month?" Tithing has to come from within, from the heart. It should be done out of love.

You should see David when he speaks to children in the "I Have A Dream" program. They are mesmerized, soaking in every word. These are underprivileged children, mostly from one-parent homes, some with parents on drugs or in jail, and the only male figure they might get to see are their coaches or their mother's acquaintances or even drug dealers. The drug dealers are in the neighborhoods, recruiting these boys with their easy money, and the boys are listening, so we need to send them another voice.

Every year I have a pool party for them at our house, or take them to an amusement park. I also go to the school and talk with them. I'm like a room mother or mentor. They behave most of the time, but when they start acting up, the coordinator always notifies their parents *and* me. I let the parents know I'm holding them responsible for their children. We try to convey our love to the children, and all we ask is that they be good scholars, come to monthly meetings, and cooperate with their coordinators. Overall, we have a lovely group of students.

DAVID I always stress education. It's one thing to tell the children it's important to go to school, but it's entirely another matter to say, "I'm willing to put my money where my mouth is. This is how important education is to me, and I think it should be that important to you."

I take being a role model seriously. It's something I have to deal with whether I always like it or not. I'm an example, and these kids are looking up to me. They emulate what I do. So it's an incredible opportunity for us to be good examples.

FREDA Some athletes grumble that they didn't ask to be role models, but they are, whether they want to be or not. They didn't refuse the position, the status, or the money. All these other demands go along with your celebrity status. They no longer have a private life. Sometimes it's unfortunate, but it's one of the costs of stardom.

Some athletes say, "It's not in my contract." Okay, it's not in your contract. But aren't these fans paying the money that allows the team to give you that contract? So in a sense, you *do* owe the public—to display a character worthy of recognition. I'd like to think you'd *want* to give society that. You can call your fans crazy and silly, but they love you and what you do. So, sure, they're offended when you do something stupid, because most of them have small children who will pattern themselves after you, whether you're good or bad. I want my children to pattern themselves after someone with a good character. I don't care how talented you are, if you have no character, I don't want my children emulating you.

I always tried to be an example for my children, but I never knew David looked up to Ambrose and me as his role models. I was moved to hear him say that. I don't think parents set out to be their children's hero or role model. They'd like to think that, but when their children say it, it's a nice compliment.

DAVID When I became a born-again Christian, I learned that was God's calling for me. I have a responsibility to put it out on the floor every night and be the best I can be. This is the way I minister to people right now. People have watched me grow and change over the years. They've seen the difference in the way I've focused on the game and become more dedicated.

If I hadn't become a basketball player, I'd still probably be in the Navy, doing my civil engineering. Maybe I would have gone back to school, tried to get a master's or Ph.D. I had a whole lot of opportunities open to me because I did finish school and I did give myself the best worst-case scenario. Now, when basketball is over, I'll get involved in some type of ministry. That's what the Lord has put in my heart. I could spend

219

the next few years working with the charitable foundation. The Lord is preparing my brother to preach. I don't see him preparing me to preach. I love to teach. I love to speak. I don't know what he wants me to do, but wherever he takes me, I'm going.

My parents suggest the Lord saved my life when I was six months old so I could minister to many through basketball. That might be true. I don't know what the Lord's purpose is, but I know he saved me for a reason. I've accomplished a lot in my basketball career now, but maybe there's so much more out there, it'll dwarf what I've accomplished. But I have a peace inside because I know he's smiling on what I'm doing, on my faithfulness.

Part Six

Grandparent Years: Coming Full Circle

Chapter Forty-Eight
Dealing with Grown Children

Parenthood does not end even when children grow up and move out. But it's time to move from coach to teammate.

David Robinson is thirty years old, a multimillionaire, a world-famous star, a husband, a father. But he still seeks out his parents' advice, and they still impact his life daily, on both a personal and professional basis.

The Robinson Group isn't just family, it's business. David's parents and cousin helped him choose an agent and team, and he had so much faith in their judgment, he let them pick out his condo sight unseen, and didn't see the house they chose for him until just before closing. When he asked them to help him get established in San Antonio, they made their advisory role official by forming The Robinson Group in April 1988.

Ambrose, TRG's president, directs marketing and business development. Freda, TRG's executive vice president, takes care of David's schedule, appearances, and publicity. Cousin Aldrich "Mitch" Mitchell, TRG's senior vice president and a Stanford economics graduate, oversees financial management. Noel Hudspeth, TRG's office manager, handles the fan club and fan mail. They work in conjunction with David and his agents, who negotiate basketball and national endorsement contracts. TRG has worked with a few other Spurs, but its primary business is

David Robinson, and practically all correspondence, requests, and proposals are filtered and screened by TRG.

The 2,700-foot condo was supposed to be an investment and a place for visitors to stay, but David fell in love with it—and instead gave his parents the 6,000-square-foot house in a guarded-gate community. It was, he figured, small payback for the best parents he could imagine.

DAVID I asked my parents to come to San Antonio for my rookie year, and it's proven to be a great decision. I knew my professional career was a big part of my dad's dreams. He had talked many times about how, if he had had the opportunity to play college basketball, he would have been a great professional player, and it was obvious to me that was something he always wanted to do. I knew he would enjoy my career, and I wanted him to be there if he wanted to be there. I didn't know how much involvement they wanted to have. Chuck and Kim were just as big a part of their life as I was, so I didn't know how long they would want to do this NBA thing. They could do it as long as they wanted. I couldn't anticipate they'd love San Antonio so much. The lifestyle, the pace of life, is so different from Northern Virginia.

The Robinson Group was a group idea. And who better to have looking over your shoulder than your parents? They review contracts, research opportunities, and handle my schedule and finances. They are very good at what they do.

I could never repay them for how much they've invested in my life. Giving them money wouldn't do nearly as much as providing an opportunity for them to realize some of their own dreams. I know my dad. He wants to work. He wants to do things. He doesn't want his son just giving him stuff. He wants to plot his own way, do his own thing. So if I could help make his dreams come true, I was more than happy to do that.

Their role in my life is still very, very important. I don't think I've ever lost the need for counsel. These are people I can trust, people I've trusted my whole life. Why should it be any different now? As much as I like my agents, the bottom line on all agents is business. I know my mom's heart, and I trust it. A lot of times, she'll suggest appearances I don't feel I have time for or feel I really want to do, but I trust in the fact she thinks something's good for me. I could spend the rest of my life trying to pay them back for what they've done for me as parents, and it would never be enough.

FREDA Parenthood does not end when children grow up and move out. Even when children are independent and mature, we as parents still worry about them and want what is best for them. There is an old saying that when children are small, they are around your feet, but when they become grown up, they are around your heart.

From the moment they are placed in your arms, you dream for them, but as they grow, they begin to dream their own dreams. For better or worse, children rarely turn out the way parents dream they're going to. What *you* think is right for them may not be. We imagined our oldest son becoming a doctor or physicist, and he ended up a pro basketball player. We imagined our youngest son becoming a good ballplayer and scholar, and he's in the military, studying to become a minister. We imagined our daughter becoming a nurse, and now she is working on a doctorate in adult education. Realize these are your dreams, not theirs. Parents need to let their children choose their own careers, even if they don't seem suitable. All you can ask is this: "What do you want out of life, and how are you going to get it?"

If you voice your concerns too strongly, children will take them the wrong way and problems will occur.

AMBROSE That can lead to a communication gap, which frequently leads to friction. We need to know when to lay off. We try to refrain from commenting on our children's personal habits or physical appearance unless we are asked. If they don't ask, we shouldn't be telling our grown daughter which types and colors of clothes to wear, or telling our sons how they should cut their hair. And we should never say, "I told you so."

Even though our policies, lifestyles, and values may be similar, the generation gap is real. We try to enjoy what we have in common: the Bible, parenthood, hobbies, computers, music, and sports. We try to treat our children as equals. Often, we ask for their opinions and assistance. Only a grown son you respect can convince his dad not to refurbish his old '79 Bonneville just for the sake of memories. Only a grown daughter can convince her mom that a certain outfit doesn't become her.

We did our best as parents, and most of our mistakes resulted from loving too much rather than too little. As your children grow up, guilt over the past should be the first thing you throw away. A healthy relationship with grown children is not based on guilt or fear, but on love and caring. To banish the guilt, tell yourself you did the best you could given your resources at that time. Guilt is counterproductive; you can't change the past. If you don't like the way you handled something in the past, try to replace the guilt with simple regret and move on.

FREDA We are a kissing family. My children always told me, "You're the best mom." And when they call me now, they always tell me, "I love you." I can go over to David's house now and when I leave, he always hugs me and kisses me, even though we usually see each other two or three days a week.

But I purposely don't run to their home all the time because I don't think it's good. It's called trying to be a good mother-in-law. He has a wife and children now. You forsake everything else for your family. Mother is no longer No. 1. She's down the road. A man should serve his wife. She should be No. 1. This is straight out of Genesis 2:24 and Mark 10:7–8: "For this reason a man will leave his father and mother and be united to his wife, and the two will become one flesh." And he does that, and I like that in him. He adores Valerie. She is a good wife, a good mother, and a good daughter-in-law. She's beautiful inside and outside. She's the other daughter we never had, and we feel blessed to have her in our family.

David faces a hectic schedule—eighty-two regular-season games, not to mention preseason and postseason games and the

All-Star Game—that often takes him out of town. That's why he tries to spend as much time with his family as he can and why we are considerate of his time, even when it involves discussing business. Parents need to know when to visit and when not to visit.

AMBROSE Creating a new family is a child's ultimate act of independence. Even when we choose to pay some of the bills, we don't have a right to call the shots. We maintain this stance: We are always here to help, but we are confident our adult children can make it on their own. Now that they are adults, we have moved from being the coach to being a player on their team.

Chapter Forty-Nine

Dealing with Grandchildren

Offer advice only when asked, and never undermine the parents in front of the grandchildren.

It was dinnertime, and David Jr. was being difficult. Not particularly obstinate for a typical two-year-old, but unacceptable for a Robinson.

His daddy lifted little D.J. from his own chair, plopped him in his daddy's lap, and told him he would finish his food. The fork in his mouth and the tone in his dad's voice suggested to D.J. that it would be a good idea to start chewing, and he did.

And that was the end of that.

David Robinson's approach is usually a little softer than his dad's, but often just as strict. He believes wholeheartedly in discipline and spanking and the child-rearing methods his parents established long ago, and he does not plan to deviate from them as he and Valerie raise David Jr. and Corey Matthew.

But whatever the method, Ambrose and Freda vow not to interfere. They suggest that watching your children raise your grandchildren is like watching coaches teach your children. Fight that irresistible urge: Don't interfere. Do be supportive. These top the list of Do's and Don'ts of grandparenting.

FREDA David is always considerate of others and has a unique way of getting his point across. When little David does something wrong, he calls to him in a whisper, "Now, David, that's unacceptable. Don't do that." And that soft voice works so well, it's amazing. I think I've heard him raise his voice once. He uses almost the same tone he uses when he's pleased, but he still gets little David's attention. He believes in trying to make the child understand what he did wrong.

I say, "Boy, you're not like your daddy." Ambrose didn't have a soft voice. No, no, no, no! They'd see a face being made at them, and when he told them something, they knew exactly what he meant.

AMBROSE I didn't yell very much, but when I did, everybody listened. I'd look at David and he'd know when I didn't approve. It's the same with my grandchildren today. D.J. will come over to the house and he'll know I disapprove of something because I'll look at him a certain way. He goes to his daddy's house and he does what his dad lets him do, including some things I wouldn't let him do. As grandparents, we are pretty soft, but not as soft as most grandparents. When D.J. comes to my house, he's just as gentlemanly as he can be. We don't put away any of our little trinkets when the grandchildren come over. We tell D.J., "Don't bother," and he knows I mean it. He'll walk over and pick up a piece and look at me and I'll look at him a certain way and he'll put it back down. I don't have to say a word.

FREDA Probably the greatest reward of grandparenting is getting to reap the fruit of your grandchildren from the seeds you planted in your children, and believe me, the harvest is great. Grandchildren are all the more reason to be careful of what we plant or instill in our children.

Becoming a grandparent is an added blessing. It's very rewarding and enjoyable for us. We have two of the sweetest grandchildren you will ever meet. We take them to church, theme parks, picnics, the zoo, and ballgames.

AMBROSE We try to spend as much time as possible with our grandchildren. We are lucky to live about twenty minutes from our first two grandchildren. It will be a different story when we have grandchildren in Virginia or Mississippi, but we'll deal with that issue when it arises. Normally, when we visit David's children, it's for brief periods. We try to have them over to our house for a day or so every week. Freda takes them to the zoo or park or just about anywhere to spend time with them. I try to play with them when they come over, and I'm looking forward to the time David Jr. can play golf. Then I will be a legitimate "baby-sitter."

We love our children and grandchildren, but we must remember to allow them to be themselves. We raised our children without interference from our parents, and we should allow our children the same privilege. We try to offer advice only when we're asked, and we respect whatever guidelines our children have set for raising their own children.

We should not and do not think of our grandchildren as our own. We fully encourage and support our children's parenting skills. It's easy to be a grandparent, because we can enjoy the grandchildren—and then send them back to their parents. And it's easy to gain acceptance and love from your grandchildren if you avoid some common mistakes. We try not to overreact to what our grandchildren say or do. In an effort to challenge authority, they will often say or do things just to see how we react. They may even say or do things they don't mean, such as refusing to give us a hug or a kiss. Unless the behavior is extremely rude or violent, we try to pretend it never even happened. If and when we are extremely offended, we won't tell them; we'll speak to their parents in private.

Above all, we don't want to undermine the authority of our grandchildren's parents. In an effort to develop a strong relationship with their grandchildren, many grandparents permit in their homes what may not be allowed in the parents' home. And vice versa. It is then the parents' responsibility to teach the children about how different rules work in different places, and about respecting adult authority. If we as grandparents neglect to honor a household rule that probably took a great deal of time and effort to establish, we're undercutting David and Valerie's authority, creating unnecessary tension, and leaving them with the burden of bringing their children back into line. If we disagree with something and we think it's appropriate to share our opinion, we talk to David and Valerie in private. We never let our grandchildren know we disagree with their parents, and we gently cut off any instigation by our grandchildren by telling them what is allowed in their house does not mean it is acceptable behavior elsewhere.

One thing we've learned over the years is not to play favorites with our grandchildren. If we plan to take them to a party or theme park and one gets sick and can't go, before we ever leave, we make sure to set a date to take the sick one some other time—and then do it. If we buy an expensive toy for one grandchild, we make sure we buy a similarly priced toy for the other grandchild.

Chapter Fifty
Back to Basics

―――――――

*Parents must be benevolent discipli-
narians.*

FREDA Every morning when I get up and put my feet on the floor, I thank God for my blessings. I have to pinch myself sometimes and say, "Lord, you've been good to me. What did I do to deserve all this?"

All my children are good children. I'm equally proud of all three of them. I tell reporters that and a lot of times they look at me like, "C'mon, lady, this is a joke." But it's so true. It's like I tell children when I speak at schools, "I love David just like your mother loves you. You are her baby and she loves you and would probably kill for you, and that's the same way I feel."

I have a family that loves me and has always been there for me. My entire life has been a prime example of answered prayers. It is no coincidence that David met and married Valerie. It is not luck that all three of our children went to college and finished. It is not luck that all three are self-sufficient and love and care about each other. It is a blessing.

Ambrose and I were instrumental in rearing them, but only by the grace of God did all this happen. We were instrumental, but we had no power. The power came from God, and I give him the praise because I know only through him are we where we are today. I hope we never lose sight of that.

AMBROSE We owe an awful lot to the Lord for entrusting us with our children. We hate to think what our lives would be without them. They are there for us, and we are there for them. Raising them was a mutual learning experience. The first part of their lives, our children imitated and learned from what we said and did. But as they got older, we began to learn from them, too. We recognized each child was different and taught us something. As grandparents, we're still learning from our children and grandchildren.

Child rearing remains one of the most important things we will ever be called to do. While you might never be president of the United States or chief executive of a major company, you will be shaping the world's future with your children. Families are the basic units of society. When you have weak families, you have a weak society. Unfortunately these days, too many children are growing up with TV as a baby-sitter; they are surrounded by violence and commercials that just make them want more of everything.

As David mentioned in his foreword, childhood is no easy time. It wasn't easy for us as parents, it wasn't easy for our children, and it won't be easy for David's children or your children. I feel sorry for children who are raised by those who take their parenting responsibility lightly. One reason we wrote this book is to spread the word about the rewards of responsible parenthood.

Parents should be resourceful and help guide and encourage the children's preparation for their dreams. That is why we feel parents need a vision that will give the child a direction and purpose. Parents must be benevolent disciplinarians. Children need guidance, limits, and fences. Otherwise, they become confused. I can't overemphasize the importance of being consistent in discipline, encouragement, support, and love.

FREDA In the early years of development, a child will try to manipulate you. It is not necessary to grant all whims or wishes.

But always remember to give your child your best—real love, caring, and discipline—and the result will be a Most Valuable Person.

233

Chronology of Events

Early 1962:	Ambrose Robinson and Freda Hayes meet in Portsmouth, New Hampshire, while Ambrose is stationed with the Navy in Newport, Rhode Island, and Freda is in nursing school.
November 1962:	Ambrose and Freda marry.
May 26, 1963:	Kimberly Ann Robinson is born.
January 1965:	Ambrose transfers to Fleet Sonar School in Key West, Florida.
August 6, 1965:	David Maurice Robinson is born.
1966:	Ambrose transfers to Newport, Rhode Island.
1966:	Ambrose transfers to Key West, Florida.
December 1969:	Ambrose transfers to Portsmouth, New Hampshire.
January 1970:	Family moves to base housing in Norfolk, Virginia.
July 5, 1971:	Charles Edward Robinson is born.
July 4, 1973:	Family buys first house in Virginia Beach, Virginia.
1981:	Ambrose retires from the Navy and accepts a job in Crystal City, Virginia as an engineer consulting on government contracts.
October 1982:	The Robinsons move to Woodbridge, Virginia, about twenty-five miles south of Washington, D.C., and David plays organized basketball for the first time as a senior at Osbourne Park High School.
1983:	David scores 1320 on his SATs, makes second-team All-Metro, and is accepted to the Naval Academy at 6'7½".
April 1983:	Freda becomes a born-again Christian.
1983–84:	David grows to 6'9" by the time school starts and becomes the Midshipmen's backup center as Navy wins twenty games for the first time in school history.
1984–85:	David sprouts two inches and 25–30 pounds and blossoms into a sophomore star as Navy goes 26–6 and makes the NCAA playoffs for the first time since 1966.
1985:	After long discussions with his parents, David decides to stay at Navy even though it means he might have to spend five years after college in the Navy.
1985–86:	David becomes an All-American as a junior, setting NCAA records for blocked shots in a game, season, and career, and leading Navy within one victory of the Final Four.
1986–87:	David repeats as an All-American, sets thirty-three Navy records, and is named College Player of the Year, leading the

nation in blocks and finishing third in scoring and fourth in rebounding.

1987: Navy Secretary John Lehman announces David is too tall to qualify for a commission as an unrestricted line officer and must serve two years "restricted" duty and four years in reserves upon graduation. He says David can play in the NBA while on active duty as long as it doesn't interfere with his Navy work.

1987: New Navy Secretary James Webb says David must serve two years, but won't be able to play in the NBA even part time.

May 20, 1987: David graduates from Navy, is commissioned an ensign in the Naval Reserve, and assigned to Kings Bay, Georgia, as a civil engineer at the new Trident submarine base.

May 23, 1987: The San Antonio Spurs win the first pick in the NBA draft lottery and say they will take David despite his military commitment.

June 22, 1987: The Spurs make David the draft's first choice while he's out golfing.

September 18–20, 1987: David visits San Antonio, which rolls out the red carpet andbegins to convince David he can turn around San Antonio the same way he did Navy.

November 7, 1987: David signs a $26 million contract with the Spurs to begin in the 1989–90 season and cover eight seasons.

April 1988: Ambrose and Freda form The Robinson Group to oversee David's endorsements, financial management, scheduling appearances, and fan mail.

September 1988: David starts for bronze medalist U.S. Olympics team, averaging 12.8 points and 6.8 rebounds after sitting out a season of basketball.

December 1988: Kimberly receives bachelor's degree in marketing from Howard University.

May 19, 1989: David is discharged from the Navy.

August 1989: Chuck enters the Naval Academy.

November 4, 1989: David makes his NBA debut vs. the fabled Los Angeles Lakers and leads the Spurs to victory with a team-high 23 points, game-high 17 rebounds, and a tone-setting rejection of Magic Johnson.

1990: David is named an All-Star and NBA Rookie of the Year.

1991: David wins NBA rebounding title.

June 8, 1991: David becomes a born-again Christian.

December 1991: David marries Valerie Hoggatt.

1992: David is named NBA Defensive Player of the Year and leads league in blocked shots.

June 1992: Kimberly receives master's degree in business administration from Strayer College.

August 1992: David plays on the gold-medal winning Dream Team in the '92 Barcelona Olympics.

January 6, 1993: David's first child, David Jr., is born.

February 18, 1993: Kimberly becomes a born-again Christian.

May 27, 1993: Chuck graduates from the Naval Academy.

January 2, 1994: Chuck becomes a born-again Christian.

1994:   David clinches his first NBA scoring championship by scoring 71 points on the final day of the season.

April 1995:   David's second child, Corey Matthew, is born.

1995:   David plays in his sixth straight All-Star Game and is named NBA MVP.

1995:   David is named to his third Olympics team.

David Robinson's Web Page

Spurs Center David Robinson now has a web page on the internet. The homepage will lead you to a variety of items including opportunities to join his fan club, correspond with his parents and the president of the fan club, and give patrons an opportunity to purchase NBA related merchandise through The Robinson Group, Inc.

It will also link you to some of our favorite web sites, including local TV stations, selected San Antonio web sites, and World Wide Web yellow pages.

To visit David's homepage, use

URL HTTP://ourworld.compuserve.com/homepages/David Robinson_50

Some keywords through various search engines are David; Robinson; Spurs; and Basketball.

For further information, e-mail

75352.2300@compuserve.com

or call Noel Hudspeth at 210-696-9639.

About the Authors

AMBROSE ROBINSON retired as a Navy senior chief—one rung shy of the highest rank an enlisted man could reach at that time—after twenty years working in sonar and electrical engineering. He spent seven years supervising multi-million dollar budgets as a consultant on government contracts before becoming president of The Robinson Group, a sports management group that handles details for his son David and other NBA stars.

FREDA ROBINSON specialized in newborn nurseries or pediatrics eight of her twenty-one years in nursing, and thus can call upon a wealth of both clinical and practical experience when she suggests what works and doesn't work in rearing children. She lives in San Antonio with her husband, Ambrose.

STEVE HUBBARD is a senior writer for *Inside Sports* magazine, an award-winning writer for leading magazines and newspapers, and the author of four books. Hubbard, who has covered professional sports since 1979, lives in Pittsburgh with his wife, Julie, and his children, Katie and Zack.